SWORD FIGHTING

A Samurai's First Lessons
Published in 1897

Author
関重節治・Seki Juroji

Translator
シャハン・エリック Eric Shahan

関重郎治・Seki Juroji
1823 – 1905

Seki Juroji · 関重朗治

Outline of Seki Juroji's Life and Training

Seki Juroji was born in the 6th year of Bunsei (1823) in Matsushiro Domain, which is modern day Nagano prefecture. He began his martial arts training under his father Seki Yoshimoto.

Nagano Prefecture

His father received Menkyo Kaiden, certification of complete transmission, in Hachiman Shinto Ryu Kenjutsu 八幡新当流剣術 in 1819 from Fujikura Kosho. Fujiwara was the Kenjutsu Shihan, Official Sword Instructor, for Matsushiro Domain.

The illustration above is from an undated Shinto School document. This section of the scroll is titled *Shinto School Sevenfold Tachi (Sword) Progression.*

iv

Seki Juroji ・ 関重朗治

He received Menkyo Kaiden, or complete transmission of all techniques and secrets, in Genkai Ryu 源海流 from a man named Nishizawa Uemon. The Genkai School curriculum contained: Yawara 和 (Jujutsu) Nawa 縄 (Rope Binding) Bo 棒 (Wooden Staff,) Iai 居合 (Sword Drawing) and Tachi 太刀 (Sword.)

① 源海流 （柔、縄、棒、居合、剣）

剣友源海居士が流祖。信州に伝承した。剣友源海—吉川左門助信—小菅清哲正継（精誓斎、儀右衛門）—小松清左衛門重友—桜井清重郎正勝—宮下又右衛門光凶—② 西沢七右衛門郷式—③ 関重郎治美智—④ 関重郎治貴易。

Lineage chart of the Genkai School showing the ① founder of the school at the beginning before Nishizawa Uemon took over. ② Nishizawa then passed the school to ③ Seki Juroji's father passing it on to his ④ son.

From the *Encyclopedia of Japanese Martial Arts Schools* 1963
by
Watatani Kiyoshi 綿谷雪 (1903 - 1983)
Yamada Tadachika 山田忠史 (1923 -)

v

Later, Seki Juroji received reviewed certification in the Taiheishinkyo School. According to the *Encyclopedia of Japanese Martial Arts Schools*, the Taiheishinkyo "True Mirror of Mt. Taihei" School contains Iai, Kenpo (Jujutsu) and Naginata (Halberd.) It was founded by a Ronin by the name of Wakana Shinkyosai 若菜真鏡斎, in 1778.   Below is an example of a Taiheishinkyo School certificate from the 10th year of Tenpo 1839.

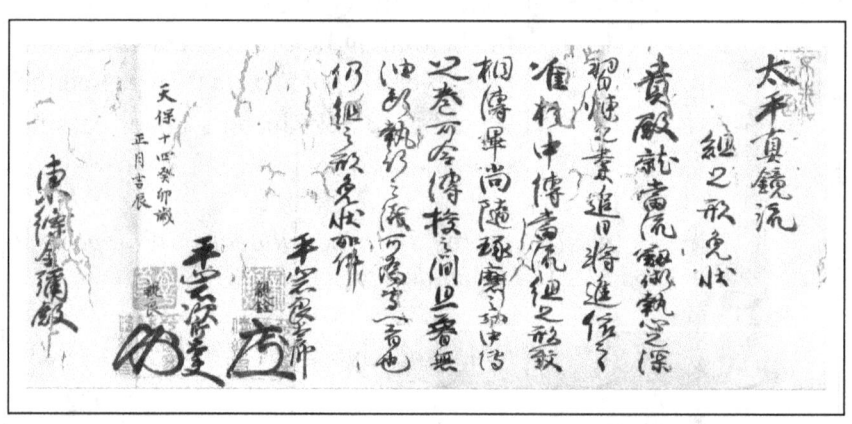

Seki Juroji · 関重朗治

Later, Seki Juroji travelled around Japan enrolling in other schools to improve his swordsmanship. He joined the Itto School and in 1854 he received the rank of "12 Rules of the Sword." Seki Juroji then returned to Nagano and opened his own Dojo in 1855. Following the Meiji Restoration in 1868, he was forced to close his school, probably due to lack of government funding, however in Meiji 23, 1890 he opened his school to private students. He died on November 17th, 1905.

Meiji Restoration and the New Ministry of Education

Following the Meiji Restoration in 1868, the government began a modern education system in 1872. Various martial arts practitioners lobbied the government to include their arts in the school curriculum. This met with resistance by the Department of Educations which was concerned with the pre-modern teaching methodology. This resulted in martial arts practitioners repackaging their art and emphasizing the physical fitness benefits along with mental training. In particular Kenjutsuka (sword practitioners) and Jujutsu practitioners sought to reshape their curricula to make them more palatable to education ministry officials.

Petitioning the Government

Seki Juroji was part of the movement to include traditional martial arts as part of the standard school curriculum. He formed the Patriotic Committee of the Brave and Just with the purpose of encouraging the practice of martial arts. The began a fundraising campaign and recruited the former Kobusho (Japanese Military Academy) instructor Sakakibara Kenkichi 榊原鍵吉 (1830 –1894) who was the headmaster of the Jikinshinkage School of sword fighting.

He sent his first petition to the government on December 19th 1893, which included the phrase,

The concept of Bun-Bu, literary learning in conjunction with martial learning, is fundamental to the make-up of this country. Literary learning is a tool for polishing the rule of law, while martial arts are a tool for establishing peace in a violent world.

He concluded this document with an overview of his proposed School Physical Fitness Program of Hachiman Shinkyo School Kenjutsu. This was a summary of the techniques in this book.

His petition was completely ignored by the government as was his second in March 1894 and third petition in December of the same year. His fourth petition, in 1895, was submitted in conjunction with other famous martial artists also initially was ignored by the ministry of education.

However perhaps due to the First Sino-Japanese War (1894 –1895) and the overall ethos of *Shobu* 尚武, or militarism. Their conclusion was not in Seki Juroji's favor. One of the reasons they gave for not making Budo an official subject to be studied at school was,

There is a chance that Gekken, sword fighting can lead to brain damage.

The government was concerned about the pre-modern teaching system and considered the pursuit of martial arts as an extra-curricular activity.

Seki Juroji's Response

Seki Juroji wrote an 11 point response to this and submitted it to the department of education.

Regarding installing Kenpo, sword fighting, as a subject and teaching it in elementary school, I would like to state that such a subject would be of no danger to the health of students.

His eleven-point refutation was as follows:

1	一、維新前ノ士分ハ，各十才前後ヨリ剣道ヲ学習セザル者鮮シ。其当時ノ士皆脳ヲ傷害セラレシヤ否哉。数年間実地，幾多ノ児童ヲ見ルニ，学校ニアリテ未タ一人モ撃剣ノ為ニ脳痛ヲ覚ヘシ者アルヲキカズ。却テ常ニ頭痛ニ悩マサルル者，撃剣ニヨリ治癒シタル例多アリ。聞ク『ベルツ』ハカセ打撃ノ結果ヲ検案シ，脳ニ無害ナル事ヲ証明セラレタリ。以テ撃剣ノ脳ニ傷害ナキヲ知ルベシ。

1. Before the Meiji Restoration, those in the Samurai class began training in Kendo from around the age of ten. I spoke with some Samurai that grew up in that environment and all of them stated they had no brain damage. Over the course of several years I talked to many children and no one could recall anyone at school complaining of brain pain due to Gekken. On the other hand, I did come across many cases of people complaining of headaches that were cured after doing Gekken. As you know the German doctor Erwin Otto Eduard von Bälz (1849 –1913) who was the personal physician to the Japanese Imperial Family, investigated the effect of Dageki, or strikes, and certified that they do not cause injury to the brain. Thus, it should be clear that the strikes used in Gekken do not cause brain injury.

2	二、腸胃ヲ壮健ニシ，脳病胃病肺病ヲ癒シ，皮膚ヲ強クシ，故ニ又随テ，学文モ進ム事甚シキ例多クアリ。

2. Gekken is good for the digestive system, heals mental, stomach and lung related illnesses as well as strengthening the skin. Due to this there are many examples of this having a positive influence on academic learning.

3	三、撃剣ハ天地ノ正気ヲ鼓舞スルヲ以テ、呼吸ノ力ヲ強クシ、胸廓ヲ拡大ニスル者ニシテ、気力胆力ヲ強健ニス。

3. Gekken serves to draw out the energy of heaven and earth. Your respiration becomes stronger and as your chest becomes enlarger your energy and fortitude strengthen.

4	四、筋骨健康ニス。

4. It improves the health of the muscles and bones.

5	五、遠路往復疾走スルモ、疲労ヲ感ズル事鮮シ。

5. When travelling a long distance down a road and back again, even if you were to run, you would not feel exhaustion.

6	六、眼力ヲ機微ニシ、己ガ目ヲ敵ノ眼中ニ置クガ故ニ、自ラ観察シ、八方ニ眼ヲ配リ、敵ノ強臆ヲ見ル事、日光ノ如クナルベシ。

6. Your eyesight will become sharper. Since you have developed the habit of looking your opponent right in the eye, your powers of observation will increase and you will become aware of what is in all eight directions (all around you.) You will be able to an opponent's strengths and fears (strengths and weaknesses.) Your eyes will shine like a ray of light from the sun.

7	七、農工商トモ、其業務に勢力ヲ強クシ、盗賊等忍入ノ際、眠リヲ早ク覚シ、其要害ヲ堅固ニス。

7. No matter what your profession, farmer, craftsman, or merchant your business acumen will increase. At the same time if a thief or robber should try to slip into your property, you will be able to wake quickly and you will be able to find a strategic position and defend yourself.

| 8 | 八　軍人トナル時ハ，其威力大ニシテ，恰モ猫ノ鼠ヲトラフルガ如シ。 |

8. When you enter military service, the force you project will surprise much stronger adversaries like a cornered rat suddenly turning and attacking the cat that was pursuing it.

| 9 | 九、　山中原野峠等，其外猛獣強賊ノ憂ヒヲ避ケ，又，乱妨人等，其術ニ恐レ手向スル事ナシ。 |

9. If you are set upon by wild beasts or burly thieves in the mountains, fields, plains, or craggy peaks you will be able to deftly evade danger.　Further, when you encounter a violent person, you will neither feel fear nor raise your hands helplessly.

| 10 | 十、　剣術ノ徳アル事ニ恐レ，疫病等ノ病ヲ受ズ。 |

10.　　Due　to　the　inherent　morality　of　Kenjutsu communicablediseases will not infect you.

| 11 | 十　足力ヲ丈夫ニシ，手ノ握力ヲ大ニシ，立居等総テ善スル事，其利益甚ダ多シ。故ニ大略ヲ記ス。 |

11. Your leg strength will improve as will your grip. Both when standing and sitting your posture will improve.　There are a multitude of other benefits I will not list here due to space constraints.

Source:
Professor Nakamura Mino 中村民雄
December 1980 *Journal of Martial Arts Research* 武道学研究

剣法体操図解
KENPO TAISO ZUKAI

SWORD FIGHTING :
A SAMURAI'S FIRST LESSONS

関重郎治
BY SEKI JUROJI
PUBLISHED JANUARY OF MEIJI 30
1897

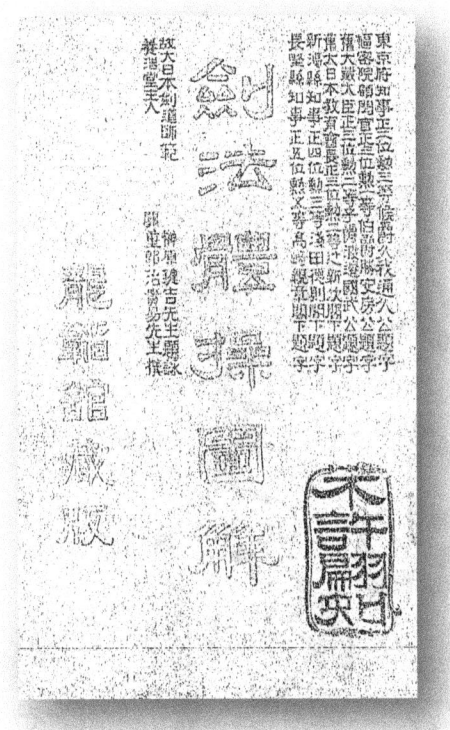

Kenpo Taiso Zukai
An Illustrated Guide to Sword Fighting Physical Fitness Lessons

Or

Sword Fighting : A Samurai's First Lessons

Introductory Calligraphy by:

- Koga Michitsune
- Katsu Kaishu
- Watanabe Kunitake
- Asada Tokunori
- Takasaki Chikaaki
- Sakakibara Kenkichi

擊剣秋風鬼
Gekken The Autumn Devil Wind

Calligraphy by Koga Michitsune
Koga Michitsune 久我通久(1842-1925)
A politician who served as the governor of
Tokyo. He was famous for his Waka style
poetry and calligraphy

活人剣

活人剣
Katsujin Ken
Life Giving Sword

Calligraphy by Katsu Kaishu
Count Katsu Yasuyoshi 勝安芳 (1823 – 1899) who is best known by his nickname Katsu Kaishū 勝海舟 was a Japanese statesman and naval engineer during the late Edo and early Meiji period. He was also a practitioner of Jikishin Kage School of Sword.

4

尚武建基
Sho-Bu-Ken-Ki
Health is the foundation of the martial way

Calligraphy by Watanabe Kunitake Viscount Watanabe Kunitake 渡辺國武 (1846 - 1919) was a politician who served as a cabinet minister and deputy Prime Minister. Noted primarily for his role as finance minister, he was also the younger brother of Count Watanabe Chiaki.

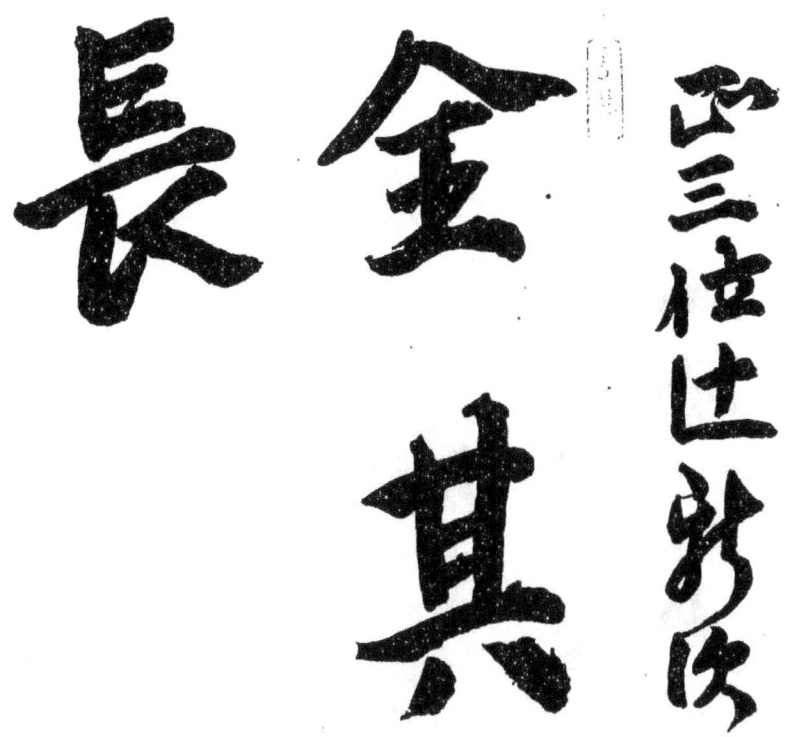

全其長

Zen-Ki-Cho

Perfect what you are best at

Calligraphy by Tsuji Shinji
Tsuji Shinji 辻新次 (1842-1915) was originally in the military and studied the construction of artillery. However, an accident at a gunpowder factory injured him and he became an educator. He became the first head of the Department of Education.

一釼答君恩

One Sword to Honor Your Lord

Calligraphy by Asada Tokunori Asada Tokunori 浅田徳則 (1848 ~ 1933) was the governor of Niigata prefecture at this time. He previously served as governor of Nagano Prefecture from 1891~1896. The calligraphy is a phrase used by Rai Sanyo 頼山陽 (1780- 1832.) Rai Sanyo was a Confucian philosopher and historian.

Seki Juroji ・ 関重朗治

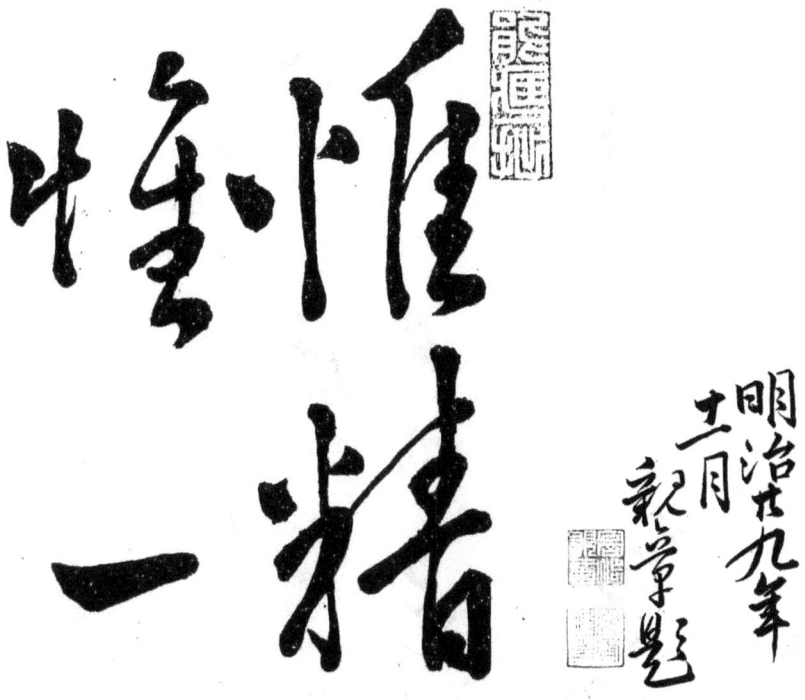

惟精惟一

This is Spirit, This is One

Calligraphy by Takasaki Chikaaki

Takasaki Chikaaki 高崎親章 (1853 – 1920) was a soldier and politician. He fought in the Satsuma Rebellion of 1877. He was governor of Ibaraki Prefecture (1893-1896), Nagano Prefecture (1896-1897), Okayama Prefecture (1897-1900), Miyagi Prefecture (1900), Kyoto Prefecture (1900-1902) and Osaka (1902-1911).

8

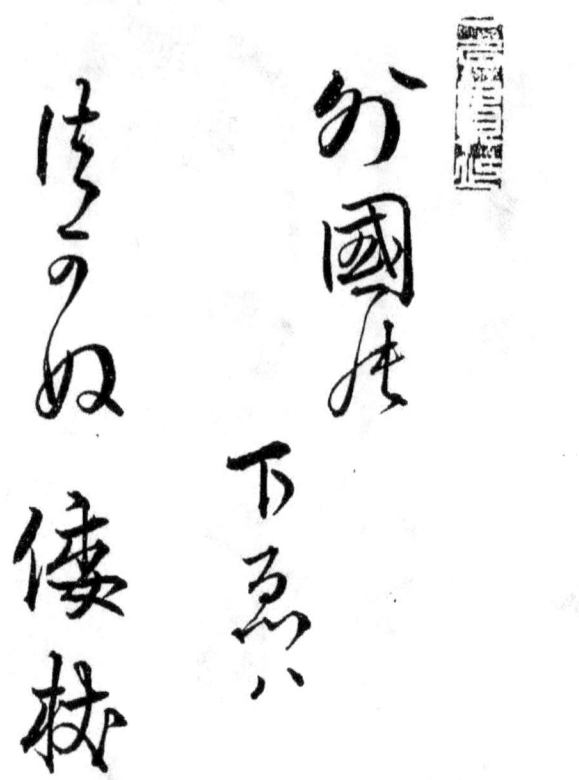

我國の下ゑは つかぬ倭杖

Our country will fall because of the useless wooden sticks

Sakakibara Kenkichi 榊原鍵吉(1830 – 1894) was the fourteenth headmaster of the Jikishinkage School of sword fighting. He taught swordsmanship and also served in the personal guard of Japan's last two Shogun. After the prohibition against carrying swords organized a group of sword practitioners and began demonstrating Gekken fencing events. The "wooden sticks" referred to in the calligraphy are Yamato Tsue, Japanese Canes.

9

Translator's Note

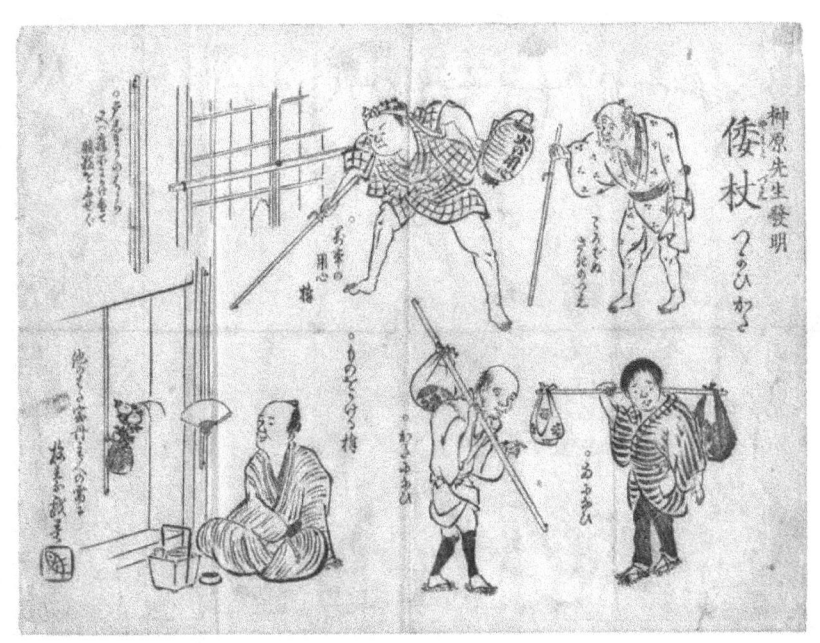

This illustration by the artist Baiso (1876) is titled 榊原先生発明倭杖 *The Yamato Tsue invented by Sakakibara Kenkichi* shows the many ways the Yamato Tsue can be used.

In the 9th year of Meiji 1876 the government banned the carrying of swords. In their place, Sakakibara Kenkichi developed a wooden sword with a metal hook. The hook served to prevent the sword from falling out. He referred to this as a Yamato Zue (Tsue,) Japanese Walking Stick in order to appease the government. Samurai began to carry these about.

Also, instead of a Wakizashi short sword they carried a piece of wood shaped like a folding fan called a Ganko Sen 頑固扇, Stubborn Fan.

自序

封建の世さハ撃劍を以て武藝の一とおし士人
の子弟を概祢成童の頃より之を修練したる素
封建の剗廢まて士人其常職を解ゝ小及んて
其業殆んと已み勞处れとも其用年猶ありび
ざるものあるも池今諸を輓近の事係ふ微するふ
十年西南の亂ふ方りて所謂瞥視隊の一聲が抜
刀を以て至る所ふ賊軍を披魔や免たるが如
きあくゝ一昨年来征清の役ふ皇軍将卒が短兵
急接の際刀劍又ハ銳槍を以て縦横無盡ふ敵人

Seki Juroji　・　関重朗治

Introduction

In the Edo Era, when Japan was under the feudal system, children of Samurai would study Gekken, or fencing. The skills they learned in that martial art would be passed on to the next generation. From a young age, students would train in this art. Though the feudal system was abolished, those skills, which were part of a Samurai's daily life, remained vivid.   However, since Gekken techniques were only known to the Samurai that trained them, they are in danger of becoming extinct.

However, as recent events have shown, those marital skills are quite important. In the 10th year of Meiji, during the Satsuma Rebellion, the Special Police Division was formed of ex-Samurai, who were all sword experts. They utilized Batto, sword drawing and cutting techniques, to cut through the rebels. Also during the Ming Rebellion last year our infantry faced close quarters combat with the enemy. They were forced to resort to swords and bayonets, felling the enemy soldiers in front, behind and on both sides.

を研斬すること貫煙したるが如き其技倆の特絶

豪快なることの云々畢竟するに封建時代み

於ける撃劔の素養なることあらん……

少く每に其餘風を受くるもの多きの為めな

ん……夫より撃劔あるもの遂に其技の

熟達と興に人をして其筋骨を強健ならしめ生體

躰を矯捷ならしめ其心膽を剛壯沈毅ならしむ

るものなるが況んや苟も高尚ある一般の兵略と

戰術とに外ならざれば鐵ひ十九世紀の今日に於

るも其素養の有無浅深は以て軍人其者の強弱

This is a true story, but how is it out soldiers possessed such skill with swords? In the end it was the last bit of momentum built up by centuries of Gekken training in the feudal era that allowed those soldiers to fight with such skill.

What this all boils down to is, people that train in Gekken stay in good health and their muscles and bones are robust. Their spirit can be best described as *A powerful warrior who never relents*. It goes without saying that they possess a general knowledge of military strategy and battlefield tactics.

In this 19th century, the relative strength or weakness of a soldier will depend on whether or not he has such a base of knowledge and to what extent.

勇怯を軼する小抦て至大の關係を有するや固とり其所あり況して今世の戰術と雖も毎獨り軍隊の操縱對抗小止らすして或る塲合み登個個實進内薄紛ミ闘亂して互に拾闘搏撃を試むるの機會多くあるに旅てハ豫しめ此技の熟練を以て此際み絶倫の技倆を示もの要あるを今猶ほ古の如くなるに抦てをやされを軍人み抦て此技の修練ハ姑く置き先つ國民体育の上よりして諸を學校躰操れ一部に加元以て適當の教授を為すハ最も切要の事みして其教授冝き

There is a correlation between whether or not a soldier has this type of training and how strong, weak, brave or cowardly they are. Considering this with respect to the way battles are fought in this day and age, a single person not up to standards will not affect the operational effectiveness of a military unit. However, there will be many situations where a soldier will have to advance on his own and engage personally with the enemy, flesh to flesh. In that one on one combat situation the soldier will be battling with weapons or even his fists. It is essential for soldiers to demonstrate a peerless technique in these situations, thus extensive training in Gekken must be done. Thus the old ways of training need to be implemented.

Placing the importance of military personnel learning these skills aside for now, the first thing needed is to include is to include martial arts that teach these sorts of skills in the school physical education program. Including classes on this subject is of fundamental importance.

劔法躬操圖解

二 前半部再版片

を得バーはめて既に二十餘年来少年文弱に傾
き此弊を濟ひ一を以て兒童を一て後来國家の
兵役に服して益す強健勇武の軍人と為らしむ
るあらん得ん是余輩同志が最も教育勅語の大
旨を体躰し國家戦勝の餘勢に乗と軍事的体育
の一法として撃劔を學校の教科に加へんこと
を望み書を文部の當路者に上り以て請ふ所あ
學問以其願意未ぎ採用せらるより玉すく
雖も其書は卓に収納し置れたるも早晩或を操
用の榮を得るの日なーん余は其當時に拔て當

17

By teaching an appropriate number of lessons in these skills students can learn the proper fundamentals. If approval is granted for these types of classes, then it will go a great way to reversing the trend over the last 20 years of students becoming immersed solely in book learning. Henceforward, this focus will allow each and every youth be of benefit to the armed forces. This will mean our army will fill with healthy, brave and strategically knowledgeable soldiers.

At the same time, I am trying to persuade the government to include this type of thinking part of the text used to describe the education system. The patriotic victory to continue this impetus to develop a method whereby the populous is given militaristic physical education. Thus, my goal is to include Gekken as a subject in school I am currently petitioning the person in charge of the department of education regarding this. While I have petitioned the government, I have no way of knowing if it will be adopted or not. I have included this book in my petition and if it is adopted, it will be a great honor.

路者の参考として剣家諸流の奥秘を参酌折衷
一最も児童躰育に適するの剣法十二形を撰み
其形容を図し且つ附するに簡単の解説を以て
し以て其顔書に添へたり此頃同志并二門人等
余に慫慂するに上梓以て世に頒たんことを以
てす因て之を名つけて剣法躰操図解と曰ひ以
て剤厰氏に附するおゝくなり世の教育に従
事もるもの幸に此冊子に由て剣法の大要を知
り而して之を躰育の上小應用せん廣教く八國
家縷急事あるも日に方り其教授を受る者も

Seki Juroji ・ 関重朗治

This book that I sent to the head of the department of education contains the secrets of many different schools of sword. We all considered the fact that this would be for use in a school physical fitness program so we compromised and came up with Kenpo Ju-ni Kata, or 12 Sword Fighting Techniques. Each of these techniques has been illustrated and a simple explanation included for each step. This is what I included with my appeal to the government.

Following my submission of my letter to the government my students along with other martial artists persuaded me to make this book available to the public. Thus I have titled this book *An Illustrated Guide to Sword Fighting Exercises,* and sent it off to a publisher. Now I am delighted to announce that with the publication of this book main principals of sword fighting are now available for study.

て能く國民奉公の本分を盡し日本男兒の面目を揚げしむるに於て亦資益する所あらん乎是を序と爲も

明治丙申の春一月望日　七十四翁養浩堂関重郎治貴昜識す

It is my fervent wish that this book is adopted by citizens and used as a means to defend themselves in case of emergency. The students that take these lessons will be of great service to our county and will serve as an example for the boys of Japan to look up to. With that wish I end this introduction.

Spring of 1897
Seki Juroji

Seki Juroji　·　関重朗治

Translator's Note:

I am not sure why but no readings are given for the Kamae or techniques so all the names are approximate. This book was part of a proposed physical education course, so if it had been adopted a version with a more thorough explanation might have been prepared.

The program consists of 7 Kamae, or stances, and 12 Kata, or sets of movements. In each illustration the explanation is divided between how each practitioner will move, attack or defend. The author refers to the practitioners as Koh and Otsu, Former and Latter. For clarity, the practitioners will be referred to as *you* and *the Attacker* in the translation. The order of the text varies from frame to frame so I have combined the text and placed the technique in order.

About the Translation

The text for each technique is split between you and the Attacker. Below is how step one of the Kata Koteage appears in the original text:

Koteage 小手揚 Raising the Hands Steps 1 ~ 2	
Your stand in Jodan and advance with your left foot forward.	The Attacker stands in Jodan Kamae and advances with his left foot forward.

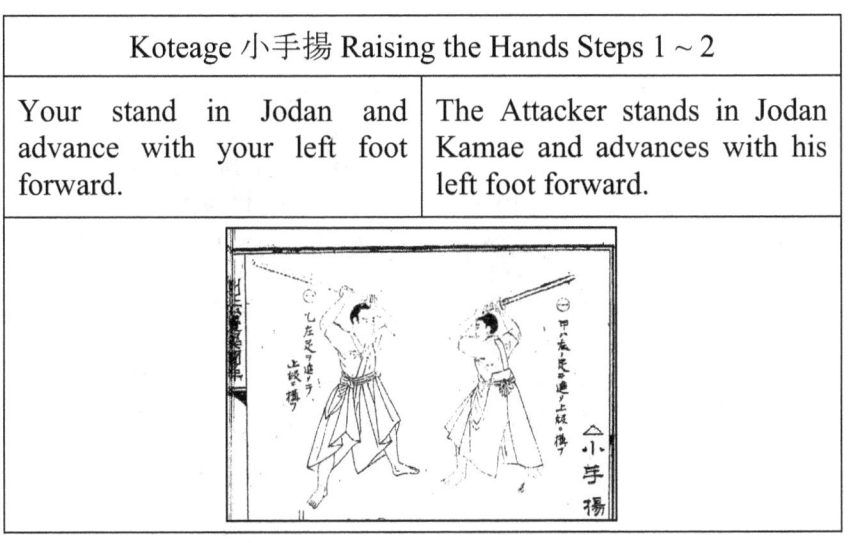

To make reading easier, I combined the explanation for each step into one paragraph.

Koteage 小手揚 Raising the Hands Steps 1 ~ 2

乙 Otsu
You

甲 Koh
Attacker

The Attacker stands in Jodan Kamae and advances with his left foot forward. You stand in Jodan and advance with your left foot forward.

In addition, are some cases where your actions occur before the Attacker's. In such cases I placed the actions in chronological order in the description. Here is an example from Step 6 of the technique Naka Seigan.

Naka Seigan 中青眼 Center Straight at the Eyes Step 6	
You then step forward with your left foot and from Jodan Kamae do a Kiri Kaeshi, Switching from Block to Cut, and cut to the Attacker's Makko, the top of his head.	The attacker responds to your Kiri Kaeshi cut to Makko, the top of your head, by stepping back with his right foot and blocking with his sword in Chudan Kamae.

乙 Otsu
You

甲 Koh
Attacker

For those cases I have placed the actions in order as shown below.

Naka Seigan 中青眼 Center Straight at the Eyes   Step 6

乙 Otsu
You

甲 Koh
Attacker

6. You then step forward with your left foot and from Jodan Kamae do a Kiri Kaeshi, Switching from Block to Cut, and cut to the Attacker's Makko. The attacker responds to your Kiri Kaeshi cut to Makko by stepping back with his right foot and blocking with his sword in Chudan Kamae.

Some of the techniques list all the actions taken by each fighter separately. This example is step 2 of Koteage:

Koteage 小手揚 Step 6	
You pull your left foot towards your right. Step back with your right foot. When the Attacker cuts up to your left hand, pull your left foot back and bring your sword to your nipple.	The Attacker steps diagonally to the right with his left foot. He steps directly toward you with his right foot. He steps forward with his left foot and cuts up from below aiming for your left hand which is holding the sword in Jodan Kamae.

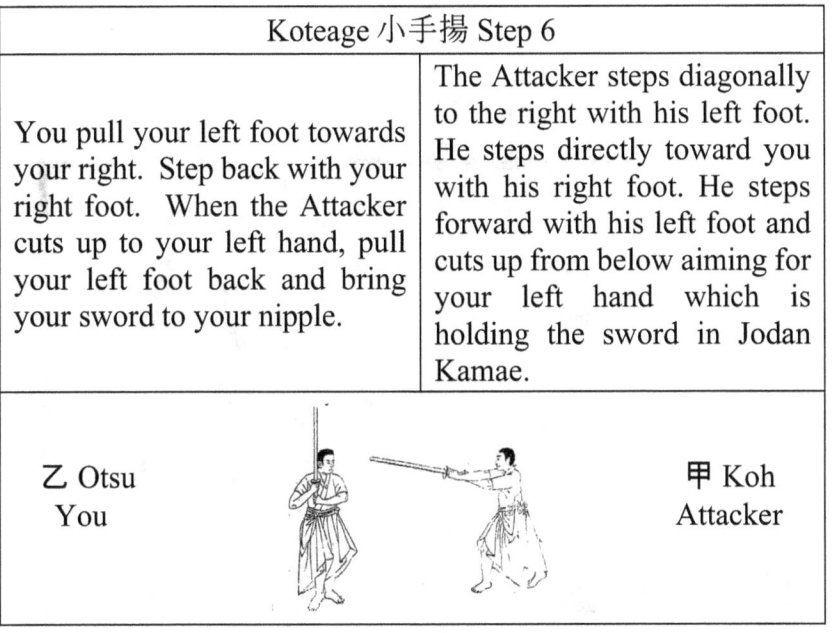

乙 Otsu
You

甲 Koh
Attacker

For this situation I have interlaced all the actions into one paragraph:

Koteage 小手揚 Step 6

乙 Otsu
You

甲 Koh
Attacker

The Attacker steps diagonally to the right with his left foot. You respond by pulling your left foot back beside your right. Next, he steps directly toward you with his right foot. In response, you pull your right foot back. The Attacker, stepping forward with his left foot, cuts up from below aiming for your left arm. You evade by sliding your left foot back and taking Chizuke Kamae by pulling your sword to your nipple.

End Translator's Note

剣法體操圖解

六歳ヨリ八歳迄。正心。眉間切。中清眼。浮

但眉間切ト浮ト八學フニ容易ナルモノ故是

ヲ初ニ教授スルモ適宜タルヘシ

九歳ヨリ十一歳迄。乳附。上啟懸。上啟廻。小手楊

歳ヨリ十四歳迄。左劍。飛龍。卦龍。真鏡

右ハ劍法體操ノ雛刑ニシテ此他数種ノ形アリ

ト雖モ幼少ナレハ是ヲ略シ只進退ノ運動太刀

ノ取扱ヒヲ慈ニシルス

Kenpo Taiso Zukai
An Illustrated Guide to Sword Fighting Drills

Outline of Training

6 ~ 8 Years Old

From the ages of 6 ~ 8 years old teach the techniques Seishin, Miken Giri, Naka Seigan and Uki.

Since Miken Giri and Uki are fairly simple to learn, they are appropriate for instructing students in the initial stages of training.

9 ~ 11 Years Old

From the ages of 9 ~ 11 years old you should teach Chizuke, Jodan Kake, Jodan Mawashi and Kote-age.

12 ~ 14 Years Old

From the ages of 12 ~14 years old teach Saken, Hiryu, Toryu and Shinkyo.

The above Kenpo Taiso, Sword Fighting Exercises, are a Hina Gata, Basic Techniques, for Young Learners. There are other techniques, due to the age of the students they are not introduced. The purpose of training at this point is to learn how to advance and retreat as well as how to handle the sword.

劍法體操シナヘ製造法

六歳ヨリ八歳迄

右袋シナヘ製造ハ中真ニ竹ヲ入マハ

リニ麥売又ハ藁ヲ割添ハ中真ヲ包ミ紙ニテ張

本綿ノ袋ニ入レ先ヘ綿ヲ入ヤワラカニ捲ヘ誓

古ノ蒟ケガナキ様ニスヘシ又コレヲ馬皮ニテ

捲ユルモヨシ鍔ハ木ニテ作リ紙ニテ張用ユヘ

シ星ヲ生徒各自ニ持参スヘシ

劍法雛形甲乙ト區別ス

甲 赤太刀

Fukuro Shinai
Padded Training Sword
How to Craft a Training Sword for Fighting Exercising

For students from 6 ~ 8 years old the Shinai should be a total of 3 Shaku in length. The blade is 2 Shaku and 2 Sun, with a handle of 8 Sun.

For 9 ~ 14 year old students the Shinai should be a total of 3 Shaku 4 Sun. This is a 2 Shaku 5 Sun blade with a 9 Sun handle.

The way the Fukuro Shinai described above is made is to first make a core of bamboo and wrap it with wheat grass. You can also make a core out of reeds by gathering them together and wrapping them in paper. Next, prepare a cotton sack, but before you insert the core in, be sure to stuff some cotton in the tip which will make the end soft. You should craft your Shinai so that it doesn't cause injuries during training. If available, horse leather will make a good covering.

Carve the Tsuba, or hand guard, out of wood and cover it with paper. Each student should craft their own Shinai and bring it to training.

剣法雛形甲乙ト區別ス

甲 赤太刀

乙 受太刀

一 雙方磬古塲ニ臨ミ左右ニ別レ互ニ一禮ヲナ
シ而メシナヘヲトリ雙方ヘ引キ別レ又甲乙
進ンデ間合ヲトル間合ハ甲乙トモ清眼ニ構
ヘ太刀ノ切先壱寸程合ヲ間合トス

31

The Two Roles When Training the Hina Gata, Basic Techniques
Ko Uchi Dachi
Otsu Shidachi

Both practitioners should enter the training space and split off to the left and right. They then bow towards each other, take up their Shinai and move to opposite ends of the training space. Both you and the attacker move toward each other until you enter Ma-ai, striking distance. What is meant by Ma-ai, striking distance, is both practitioners are in Seigan Kamae and you move until the tips of your swords are only 1 Sun, 3 centimeters, apart. This is Ma-ai.

Translator's Note: The Kanji combination Ko-Otsu means Former and Latter. In martial arts schools the Ko is the practitioner in the role of Uchi Dachi. The Uchi Dachi is typically the senior student or teacher, and is considered the teaching role. For this document the Uchi Dachi will be referred to as the Attacker. The Otsu or Latter is in the role of Shidachi. The Schidachi is the practitioner responding to attacks and performing the technique. The Shidachi will be referred to as You.

Seigan Kamae 青眼

Jodan Kamae 上段

乳戸

Chizuke Kamae

Gedan Kamae 下段

Nakado Kamae 中胴

Saken Kamae 左劍

Kuwagata Kamae 鍬形

一上段ハ太刀ノ柄鍔キハ一寸ヲ離シ右ノ手ニ
テヤワラカニ握リ左ノ手ニテ柄ノ先小指一
本ハツルヽクウ井ニ握リ又ヲ上ニ十シ頭上
二揚ゲ太刀ヨリ蒲ヽ水ノ流ル、程ニ搆ヘ左
ノ足ヲ先ニシ乙ノ虚実ヲ伺ヒ其虚ヲ撃ツ

上段

Jodan Kamae Upper Stance

This is how to hold your sword in Jodan Kamae. Your right hand should hold the sword 1 Sun, 3 cm, below the Tsuba, hand guard. Grip with your left hand low enough so that your little finger is curled below the end of the handle. Raise your sword over your head with the blade facing up. The feeling of this stance is as if water is flowing in front of your sword. Stand with your left leg forward and watch for how the practitioner in the role of Otsu is using Kyo-Jitsu, feints hiding true intent. Your job is to cut to the feint.

一下段太刀ノ持方上段ニ同シ鍔ヲ合セ太刀ノ
切先ヲ我ガ右ノ足先ニ出シ右ノ手ヲ臍ノ所
右ノ方ニ寄セ乙ノ虚実ヲ伺フ

下段

Gedan Kamae
Lower Stance

Hold the sword for Gedan Kamae in the same manner as with Jodan Kamae, except that the tip of the sword should be pointed at the end of your right foot. Your right hand should be by your navel and your right shoulder towards your opponent. From this stance judge your opponent's Kyo-Jitsu.

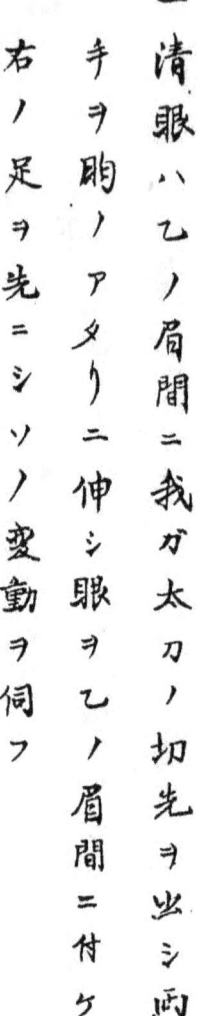

一清眼ハ乙ノ眉間ニ我ガ太刀ノ切先ヲ出シ両

手ヲ胸ノアタリニ伸シ眼ヲ乙ノ眉間ニ付ケ

右ノ足ヲ先ニシソノ変動ヲ伺フ

青眼

Seigan Kamae
Clear Eyed Stance

The tip of your sword should point at the Miken, area between the
eyebrows, of your opponent. Both arms should be extended out in
front of your chest. Your eyes should be fixed on Otsu's Miken.
Your right leg is forward ready to move in any direction at any
movement from your opponent.

37

一乳付ハシナヘヲ右ノ乳ニ付ケ踵ヲ合セテ立ツ

乳府

Chizuke Kamae
Fixed to the Nipple Stance

　Stand in Chizuke Kamae by holding the Shinai by your right nipple and bringing your heels together.

38

一左劍ハ太刀ノ持方前ニ同シ太刀ノ切先ヲ左
ノ足先ニ双ヲ上ニナシ左ノ手ヲ右ノ腹臍ノ
外ニナシ左ノ手ノ脉屦ト右ノ手ノ脉屦ト
合セ持チ乙ノ虚実ヲ伺フ

左劍

Saken Kamae
Left Sword Stance

Hold the sword in the same way as described before. The point of your sword should be pointed at the end of your left foot with the blade facing up. Your left hand should be on the right side of your waist, to the right of your navel. Hold your Shinai with the veins of your right wrist overlapping the veins in your left wrist as you assess your opponent's Kyo-Jitsu.

一中胴ハ左ノ手ヲ左ノ腰ノ辺ニヲキ右ノ手ヲ

臍ノ上ニヲキ太刀ヲ斜ニモテ踵ヲ合セテ立ツ

此他数捜ノ構アリト雖モ幼摸ナレバ之ヲ略ス

中胴

Nakado Kamae
Center Stance

Hold the sword diagonally with your left hand by your left side and your right hand above your navel. The heels of your feet are together.

There are other Kamae that we teach in this school, however since this is a guide for young learners they will be abbreviated.

40

此他数種ノ搆アリト雖モ幼拝ナレバ之ヲ略ス

劔道ハ心手足ニ隨ヒ手足心ニ隨ハサル時ハツ

イニ勝「ナシ依テ銳「ハ電光ノ如ク動カサル

「山ノ如ク身ハ飛蝶ノ如ク瞬息心氣カ一致シ

車輪ノ轉スルカ如ク滯リナク其變ヲ擊テ其不

意ヲ擊テ其虚ヲ擊テ其迷ヲ擾ヒ其邪ヲ制スル

時ハ玄妙不思議ノ心術ヲ得ベシ依テ三要三ニ

ノコトヲ忘レズ瞀古スヘキ事

Seki Juroji ・ 関重朗治

Though there are Kamae other than the ones I have introduced, this course of learning is geared towards young learners so they will be abbreviated.

Kendo practice should be done with the spirit leading the hands and feet. If you ever find your hands and feet leading your spirit, know that victory is impossible.

Your movement be like a bolt of lightning, and when you are not moving you should be as still as a mountain. You should be able to spring forward in an instant. Your breathing, spirit and marital power should be unified like two wheels on a cart. You should never become stagnant.

You should strike the opponent down when he attempts to employ an unexpected gambit. You should strike when he is unprepared. Cut his lie (feint/gambit) and allow his attacks to pass you by. Control what obstructs you by moving with the mysterious techniques held in your heart. It is important that you do not forget these three fundamentals as you train.

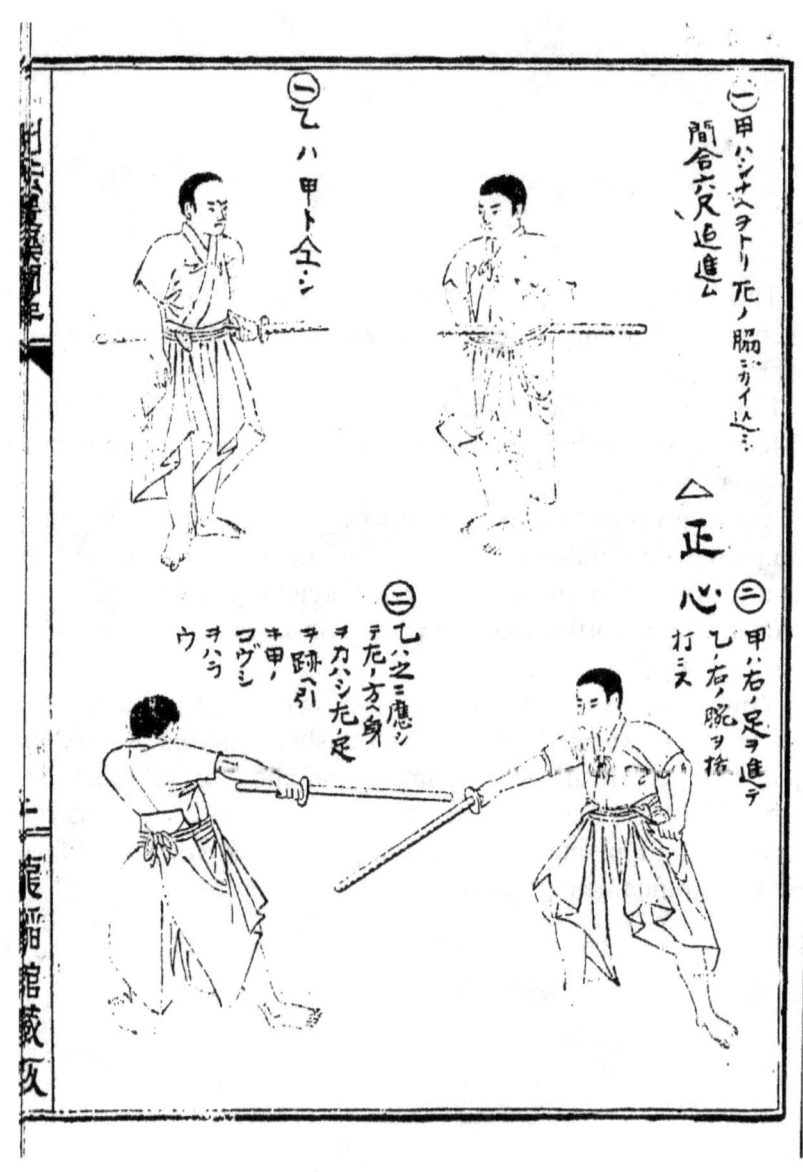

Seishin 正心 True Heart　　Steps 1 ~ 2

乙 Otsu
You

甲 Koh
Attacker

1. Your opponent stands with the Shinai by his left side. He moves forward until he is 6 Shaku, 180 centimeters from you. You move forward in the same manner.

乙 Otsu
You

甲 Koh
Attacker

2. Your opponent steps forward with his right foot and draws with a Nuki Uchi, draw and cut, aiming for your right arm. Respond by rotating your body to the left and pulling your left leg back. At the same time sweep your sword across his hand.

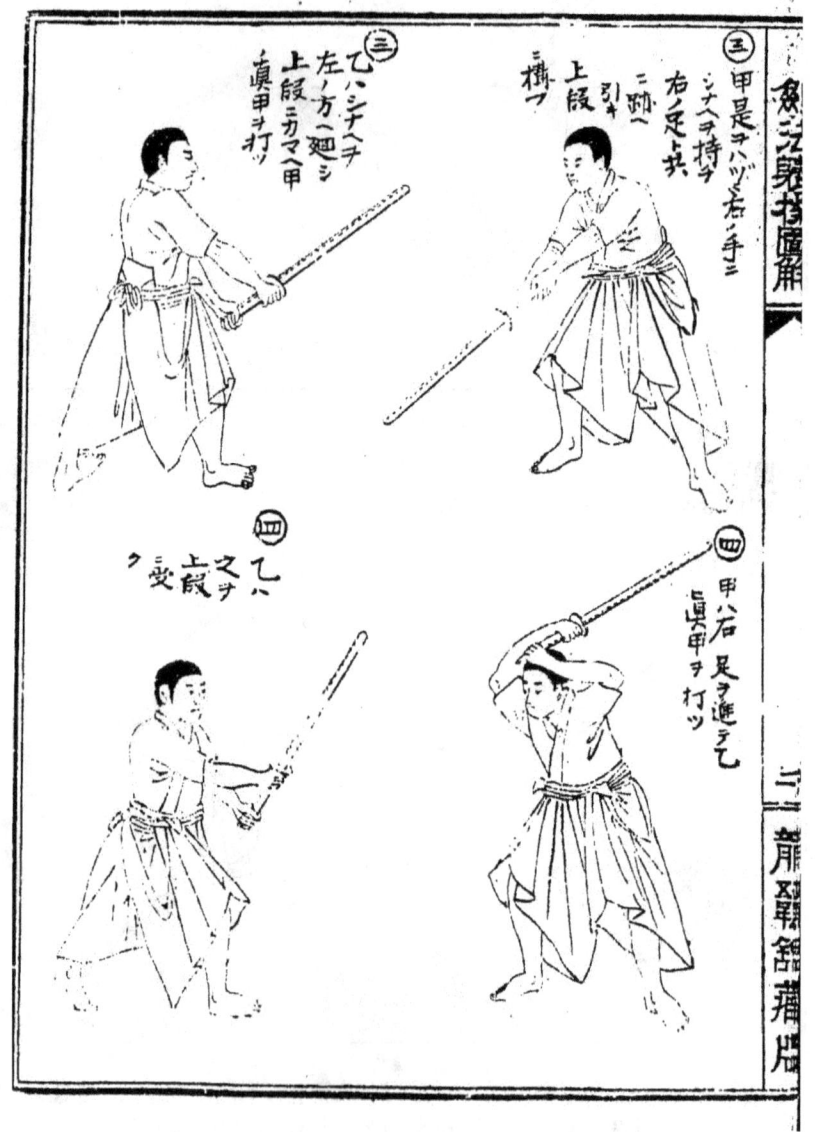

45

Seishin 正心 True Heart　Steps 3 ~ 4

乙 Otsu
You

甲 Koh
Attacker

3. The Attacker pulls his hand back slightly to avoid this and grips his Shinai with both hands. He steps back with his right foot and goes into Jodan Kamae. Rotate your Shinai back to the left and strike to Makko, the top of his head, as he stands in Jodan Kamae.

乙 Otsu
You

甲 Koh
Attacker

4. The attacker steps forward with his right foot and cuts to your Makko. Stop this cut with your sword in Jodan Kamae.

Seishin 正心 True Heart Steps 5

乙 Otsu
You

甲 Koh
Attacker

5. Step forward with your left foot and cut to Makko. The attacker defends by pulling his left foot back and blocks with his sword in Chudan. You then step forward with your right foot and cut again. The Attacker responds by pulling his right foot back and does an Uke Tome, Block and Stop, with his sword.

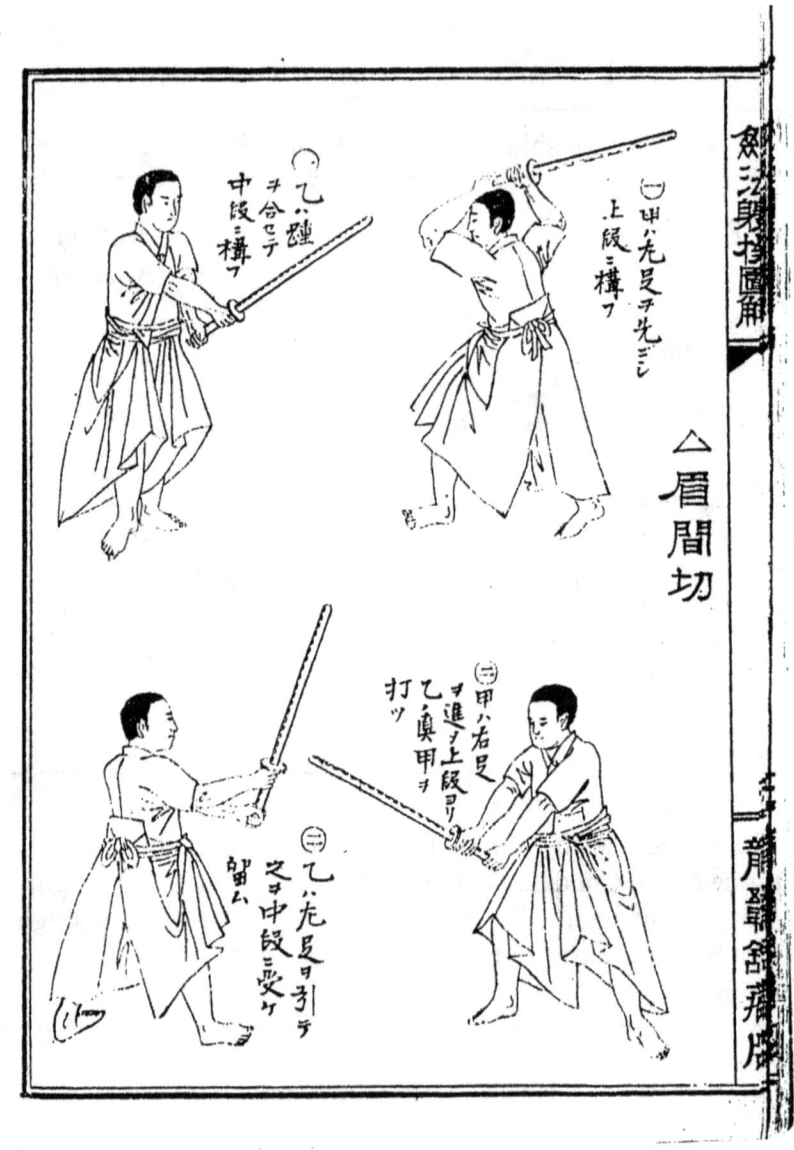

49

Miken Giri 眉間切 Cut to Between the Eyebrows   Steps 1 ~ 2

1. The attacker steps forward with his left foot and goes into Jodan Kamae. Respond by bringing your heels together and standing in Chudan Kamae.

2. The attacker steps forward with his right foot and, from Jodan Kamae, strikes to Makko, the top of your head. Respond by pulling your left foot back and doing Uke Tome, Block and Stop, from Chudan Kamae.

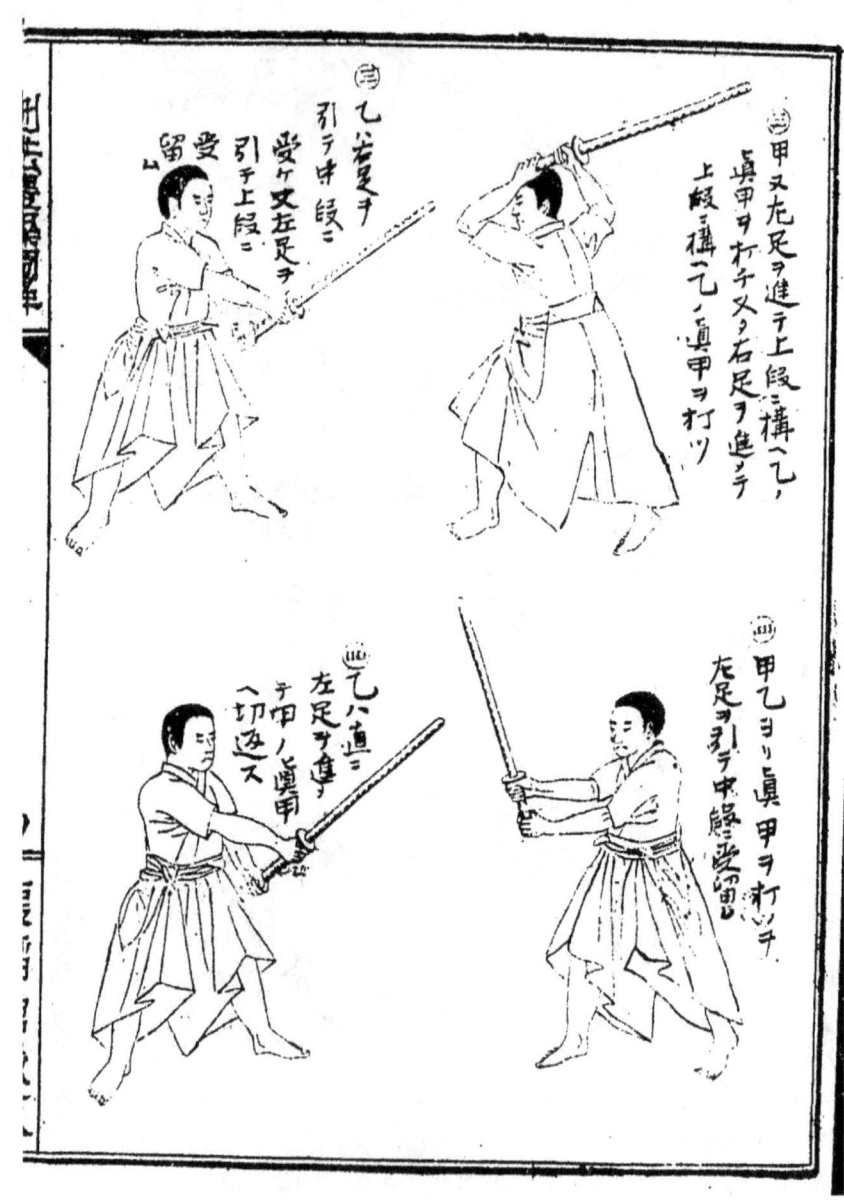

Miken Giri 眉間切 Cut to Between the Eyebrows   Steps 3 ~ 4

乙 Otsu
You

甲 Koh
Attacker

3. The attacker steps forward with his left foot and raises his Shinai into Jodan Kamae. He then cuts to the top of your head. You respond by stepping back with your right foot and blocking with your sword in Chudan Kamae.   Next, from Jodan Kamae the Attacker steps forward with his right foot and cuts to the top of your head again. Respond to this by dropping back with your right foot and doing an Uke-tome, Block and Stop, from Jodan Kamae.

乙 Otsu
You

甲 Koh
Attacker

4. You then immediately step forward with your left foot and cut to the Attacker's Makko, top of his head. This is a Kiri-Kaeshi, Your Sword Swinging From Block to Cut. The attacker defends against this attack by dropping back with his left foot and doing an Uke-Tome from Chudan Kamae.

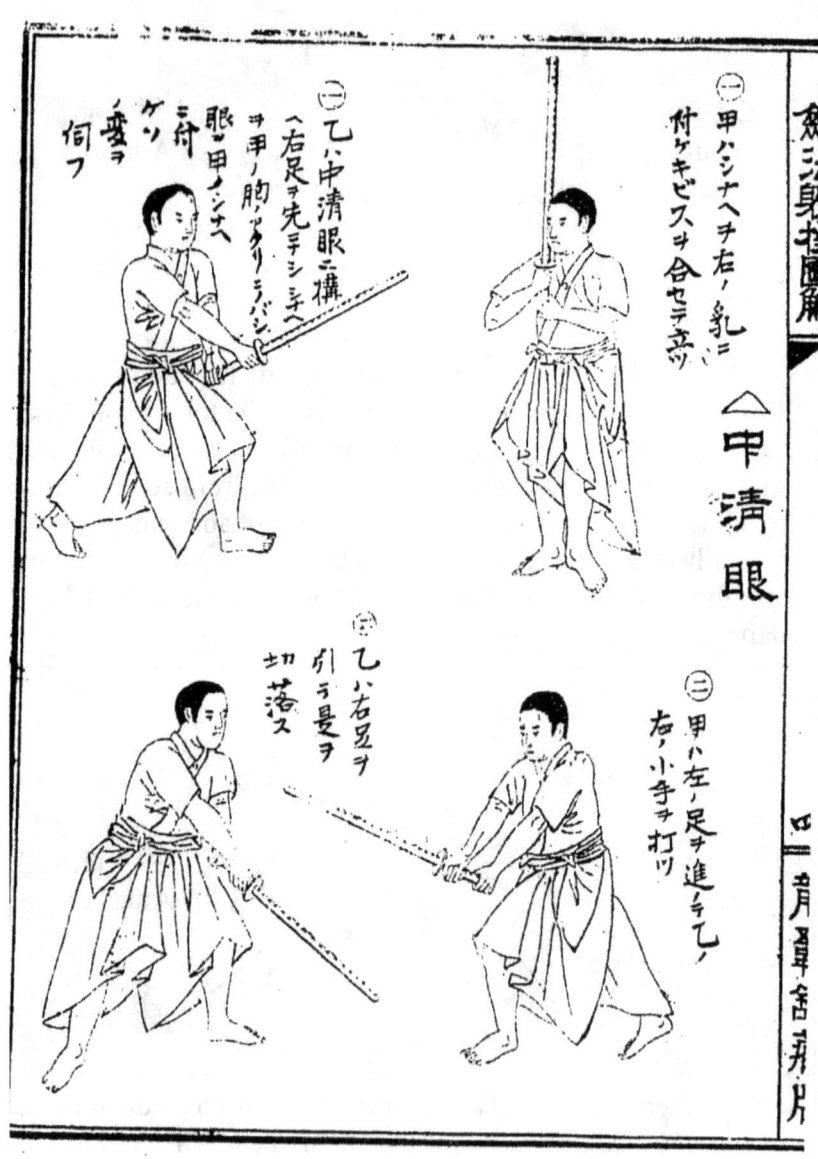

△中清眼

（一）甲ハシナヘチ右ノ乳ニ
付ケキビスヲ合セテ立ツ

（二）乙ハ中清眼ニ横ヘ右足ヲ先ニシシテ
甲ノ胸ノアタリミバジヲ甲ノシナヘ
眼ニ甲ノシナヘ
三付
ケリ
ヲ愛ヲ
ヘ伺フ

（三）甲ハ左ノ足ヲ進ムテ乙ノ
右ノ小手ヲ打ツ

（四）乙ハ右足ヲ
引ヲ曼ヲ
切落ス

象二剣当圖解

四二月罩舎弟片

53

Naka Seigan 中青眼 Center Straight at the Eyes   Steps 1 ~ 2

乙 Otsu
You

甲 Koh
Attacker

1. The attacker stands with his heels together and holding his Shinai in Chizuke Kamae, with the handle above his right nipple. You are standing in Naka Seigan, Center Straight at the Eyes Stance, with your right foot forward.   Your Shinai should be extended out towards the Attacker's chest. Keep your eyes on his sword and watch for any change in its position.

乙 Otsu
You

甲 Koh
Attacker

2. Your attacker steps forward with his left foot and strikes to your right Kote, or Hand. You respond by pulling your right foot back and striking the Attacker's sword with a Kiri Otoshi, Cut and Drop.

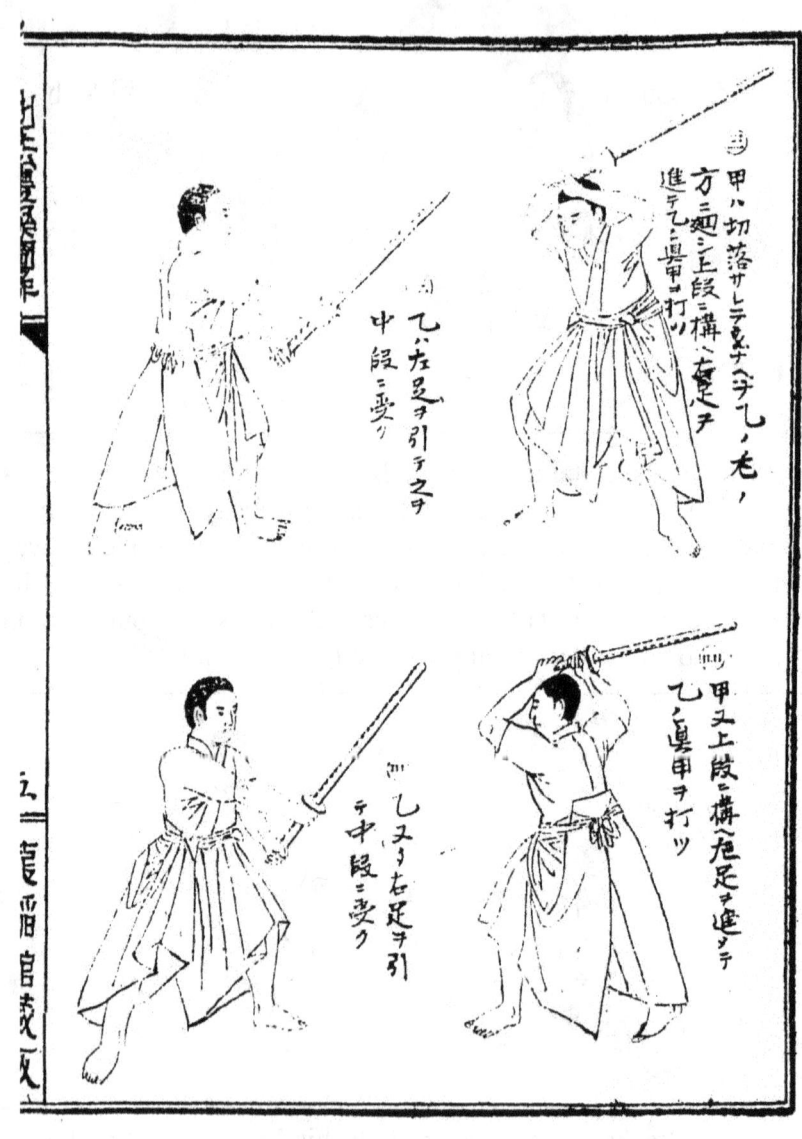

Naka Seigan 中青眼 Center Straight at the Eyes   Steps 3 ~ 4

乙 Otsu
You

甲 Koh
Attacker

3. After having his Shinai knocked down, the Attacker rotates it to the left and then up into Jodan Kamae. He then steps forward with his right foot and cuts to Makko, the Top of Your Head. Respond by stepping back with your left foot and blocking with your sword in Chudan Kamae.

乙 Otsu
You

甲 Koh
Attacker

4. The Attacker steps forward with his left foot and cuts to Makko. Respond by stepping back with your right foot and blocking with your sword in Chudan Kamae.

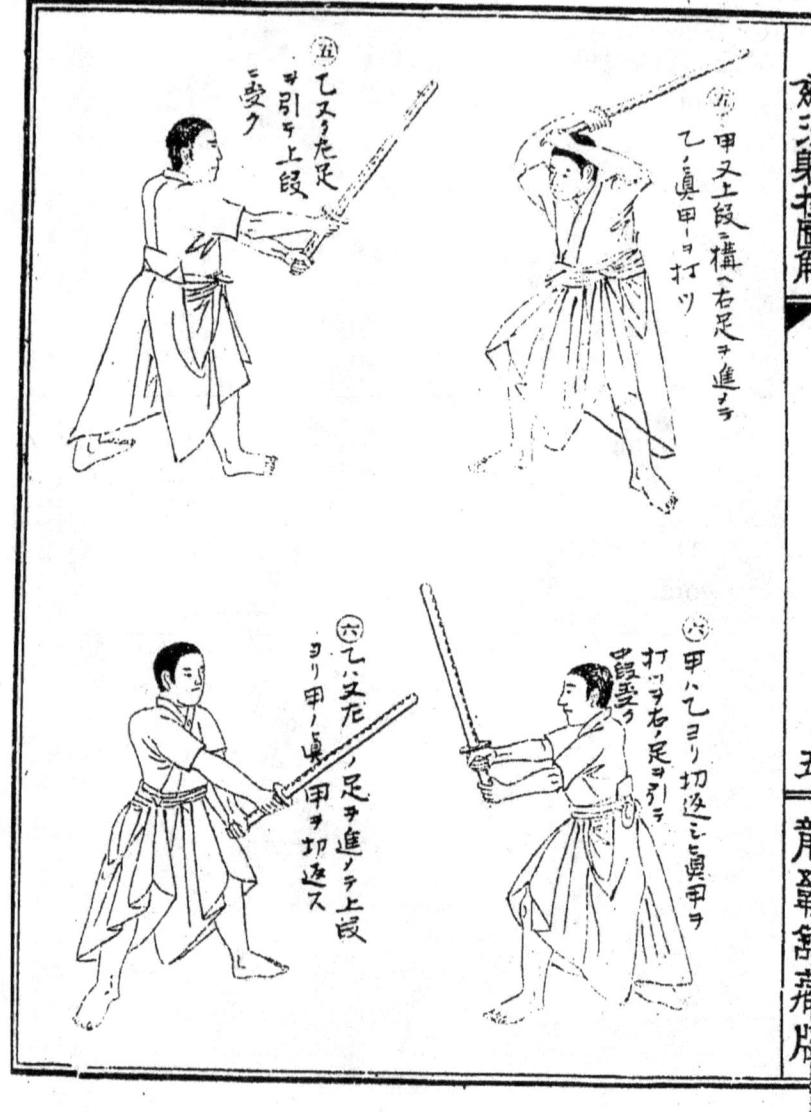

Naka Seigan 中青眼 Center Straight at the Eyes   Steps 5 ~ 6

乙 Otsu
You

甲 Koh
Attacker

5. Once again the Attacker goes into Jodan Kamae, steps forward with his right foot and cuts to Makko. You respond in the same way as before, stepping back with your left foot, but block with your sword in Jodan Kamae.

乙 Otsu
You

甲 Koh
Attacker

6. You then step forward with your left foot and, from Jodan Kamae, do a Kiri Kaeshi, Switching from Block to Cut, and cut the Attacker's head. The attacker responds to your cut by stepping back with his right foot and blocking with his sword in Chudan Kamae.

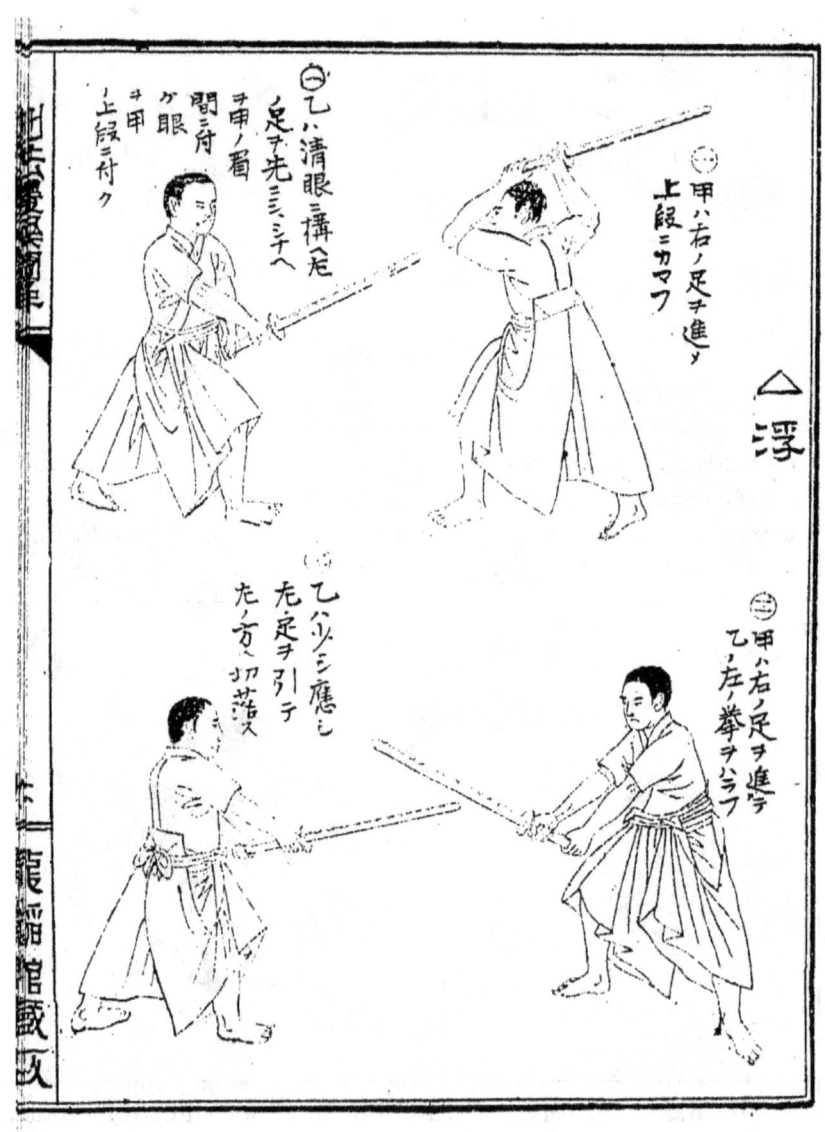

乙 Otsu
You

甲 Koh
Attacker

1. The Attacker moves forward with his right foot from Jodan Kamae. You are in Seigan Kamae stepping forward with your left foot. The end of your Shinai should be pointed at the Attacker's Miken, the spot between his eyebrows. Your eyes should be on your opponent's sword, which is in Jodan Kamae.

乙 Otsu
You

甲 Koh
Attacker

2. The Attacker steps forward with his right foot and does a Harau, or sweeping cut, to your left hand. You respond by pulling your hands back slightly and taking one step back with your left foot. Knock the Attacker's sword down with a Kiri Otoshi, Cut and Drop Strike, to the left.

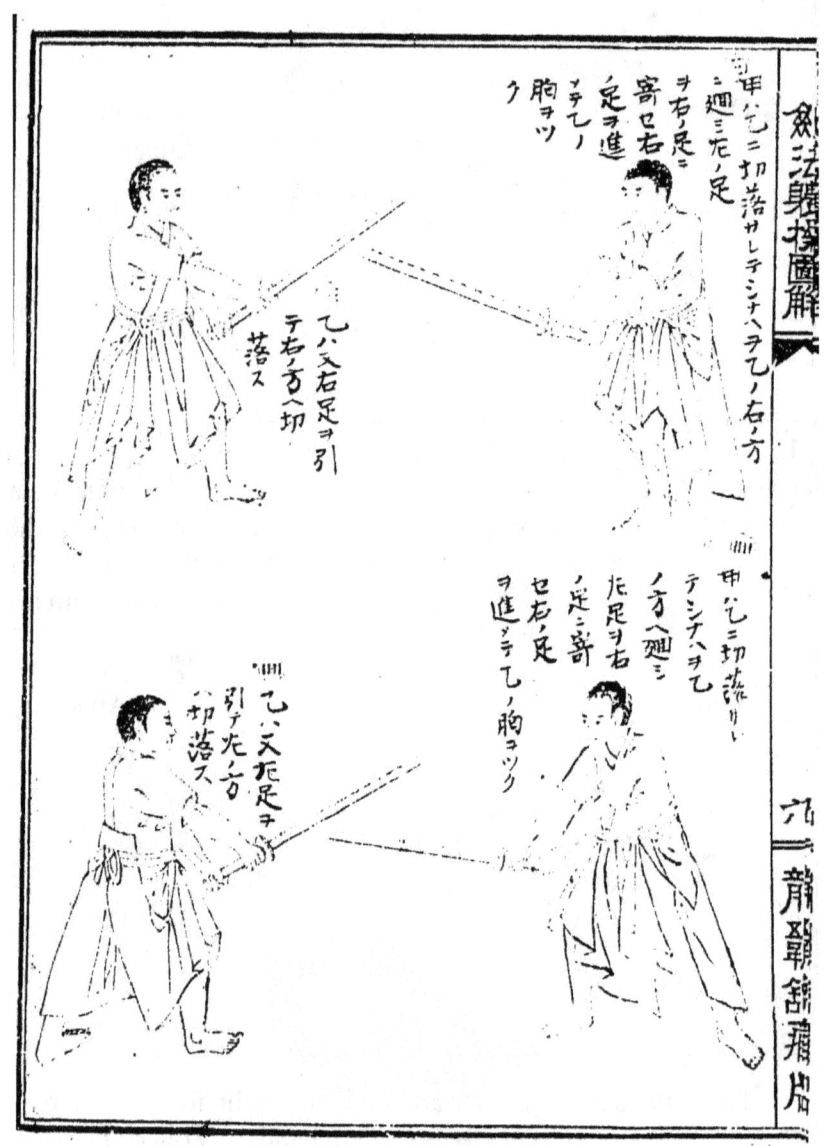

Uki 浮 Floating　Steps 3 ~ 4

乙 Otsu
You

甲 Koh
Attacker

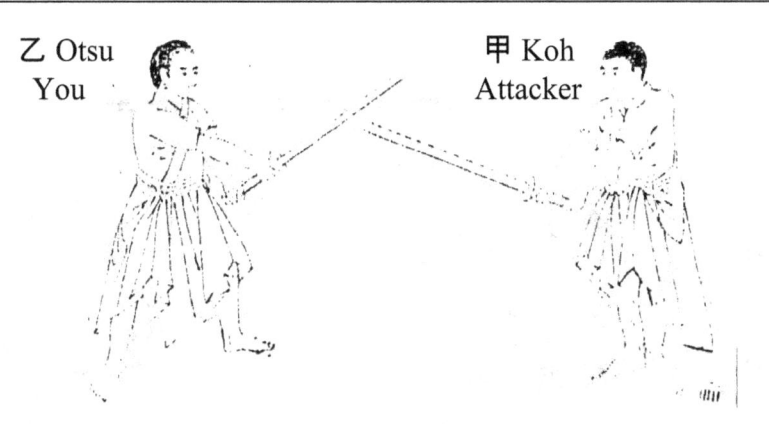

3. The Attacker responds to having his sword knocked down with Kiri Otoshi by rotating his Shinai around towards your right side. He slides his left foot up beside his right before stepping forward with his right foot and stabbing you in the chest. You respond the same way as before, except this time you step back with your right foot and defend with a Kiri Otoshi to your right.

乙 Otsu
You

甲 Koh
Attacker

4. In response to your Kiri Otoshi, the Attacker rotates his Shinai towards you. He then draws his left foot towards his right and steps forward with his right foot, stabbing you in the chest. You respond as before, by stepping back with your left foot and doing a Kiri Otoshi, this time to the left.

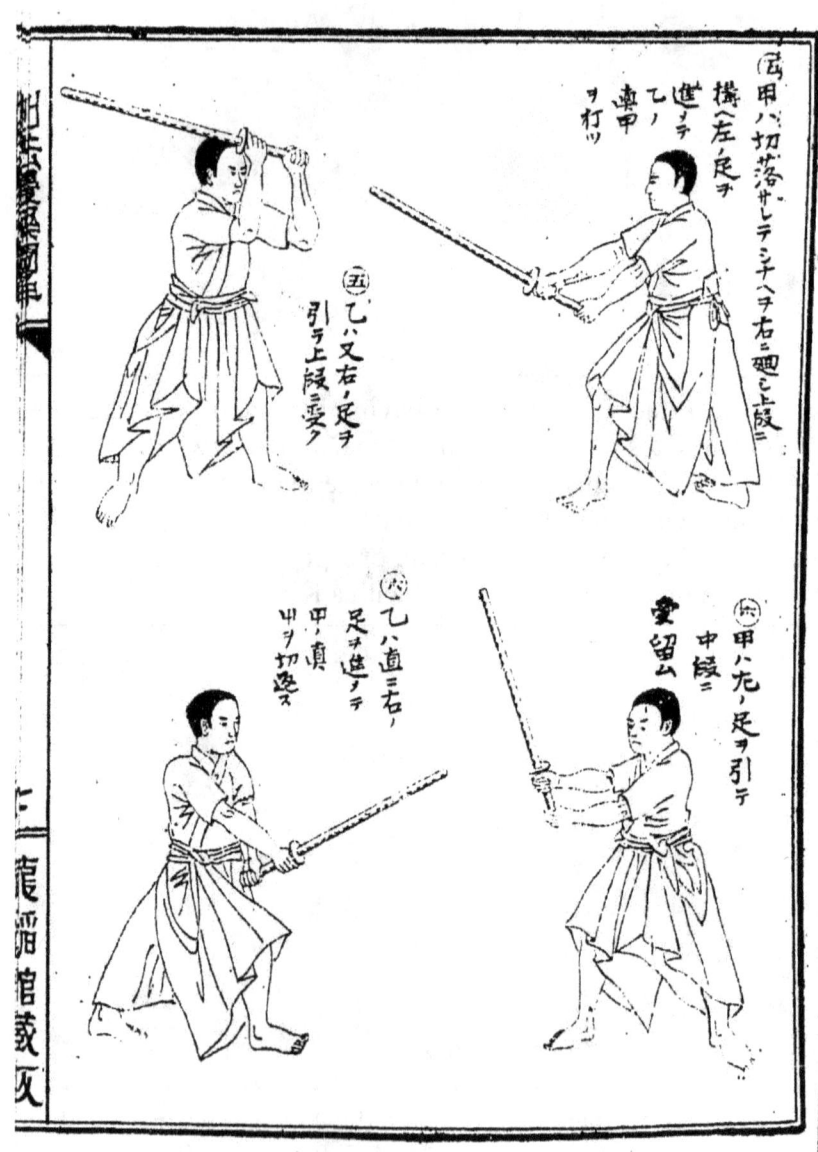

（四）甲ハ切落サレテシナヲ右ニ廻シ上段ニ
構ヘ左ノ足ヲ
進メテ乙ノ
裏甲
ヲ打ツ

（五）乙ハ又右ノ足ヲ
引テ上段ニ受ク

（七）甲ハ尤ノ足ヲ引テ
中段ニ
愛留ム

（六）乙ハ直ニ右ノ
足ヲ進メテ
甲ノ頂
甲ヲ切落ス

Uki 浮 Floating　Steps 5 ~ 6

5. You have knocked the Attacker's Shinai down with Kiri Otoshi. The Attacker recovers his sword by rotating it to the right and bringing it up into Jodan Kamae. He steps forward with his left foot and cuts to Makko, the top of your head. You respond by again dropping back with your right foot and stopping the Attacker's strike with your sword in Jodan Kamae.

6. After stopping the Attacker's strike from Jodan Kamae, step forward with your right foot and execute a Kiri Kaeshi, switching from defensive block to offensive cut, and cut to the Attacker's Makko. The Attacker steps back with his left foot and does a Uke Tome, Block and Stop, with his sword in Chudan Kamae.

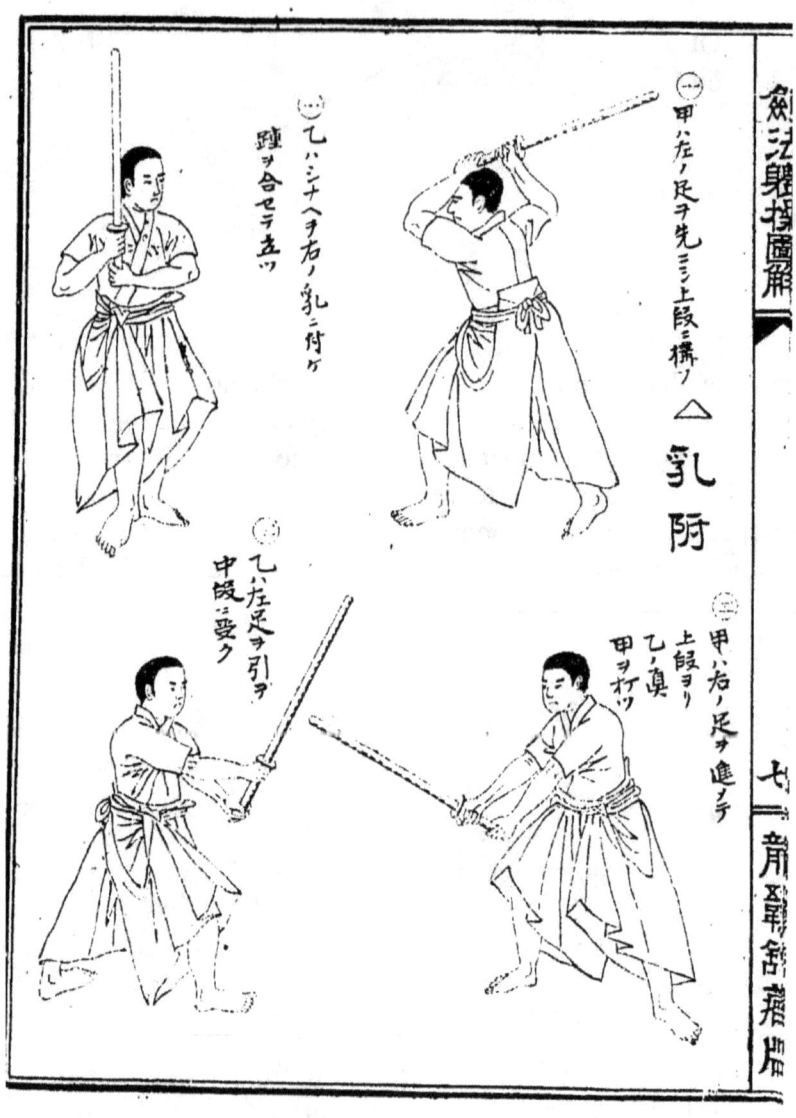

Chizuke 乳附 Fixed to the Nipple Stance   Steps 1 ~ 2

1. The Attacker stands in Jodan Kamae with his left foot forward. You stand with your Shinai, practice sword, on your right nipple. The heels of your feet should be together.

2. The Attacker steps forward with his right foot and cuts to Makko, the Top of Your Head. You respond by stepping back with your left foot and blocking with your sword held in Chudan Kamae.

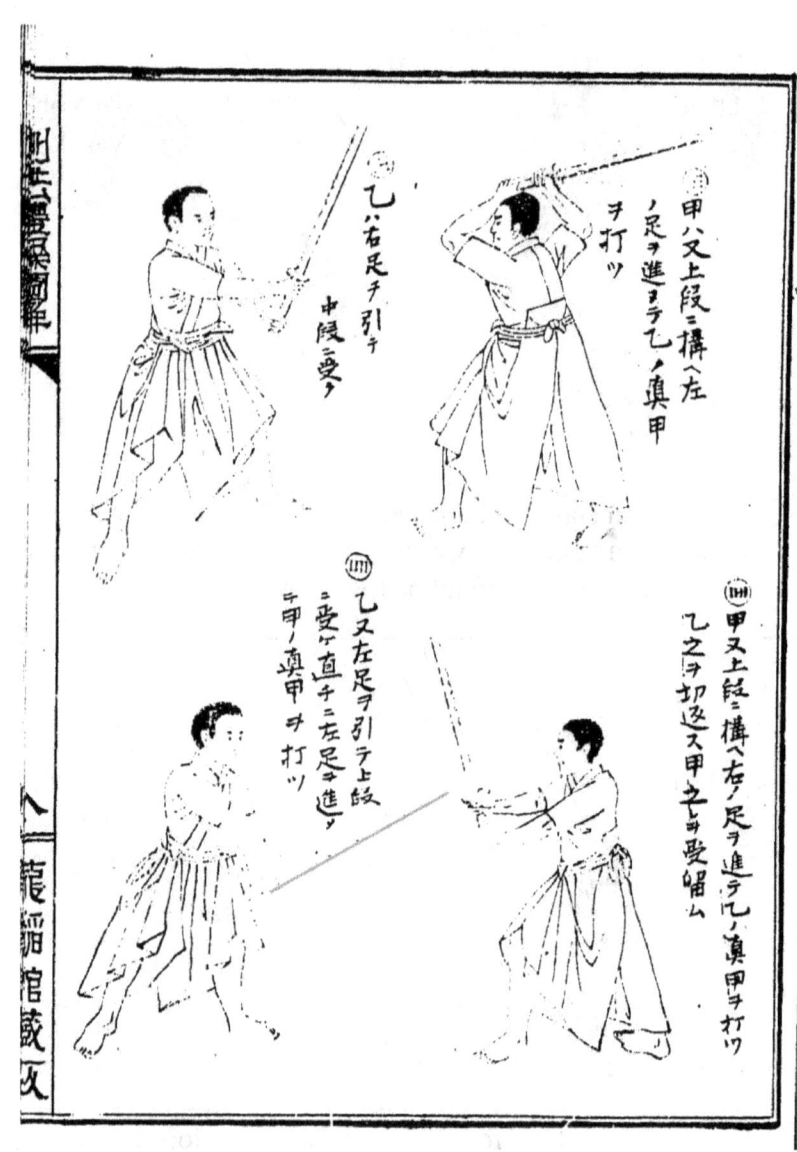

甲ハ又上段ニ構ヘ左
ノ足ヲ進メテ乙ノ真甲
ヲ打ツ

乙ハ右足ヲ引テ
中段ニ受ク

甲又上段ニ構ヘ右ノ足ヲ進メテ乙ノ真甲ヲ打ツ
乙之ヲ切返ス甲之ヲ受留ム

乙又左足ヲ引テ上段
ニ受ケ直チニ左足ヲ進メ
テ甲ノ真甲ヲ打ツ

Chizuke 乳附 Fixed to the Nipple Stance   Steps 3 ~ 4

乙 Otsu
You

甲 Koh
Attacker

3. The Attacker goes into Jodan Kamae. He steps forward with his left foot and cuts to Makko, the Top of Your Head. You respond by dropping back with your right foot and blocking with your sword held in Chudan Kamae.

乙 Otsu
You

甲 Koh
Attacker

4. Your Attacker again goes into Jodan Kamae, stepping forward with his right foot, he cuts to Makko. You again step back with your left foot, but this time block with your sword in Jodan Kamae. You then step forward with your left and do a Kiri Kaeshi, Block to Cut, to the top of the attacker's head. The attacker responds with an Uke Tome, Block and Stop.

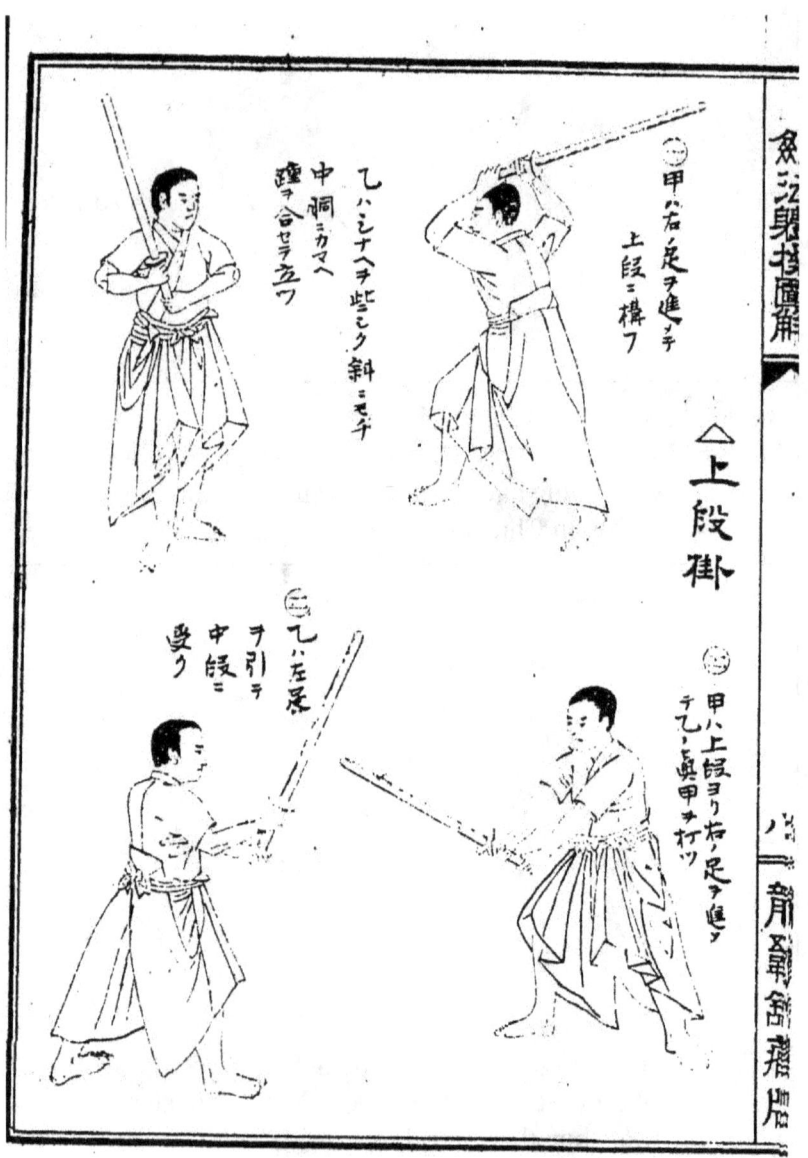

剣法興捜図解

△上段構

乙ハモナヘチ比ニク斜ニモチ
中胴ニカマヘ
蹲合セラ立ワ

中胴ニカマヘ

甲ハ右ノ足ヲ進ノテ
上段ニ構フ

(二) 乙ハ左足
ヲ引テ
中段ニ
受ク

(二) 甲ハ上段ヨリ右ノ足ヲ進メ
テ乙ト與甲ヲ打ツ

ハ前五戦舎履居

Jodan Kake 上段掛 Attacked from Upper Stance Steps 1 ~ 2

乙 Otsu
You

甲 Koh
Attacker

△上段掛

1. The Attacker stands in Jodan Kamae and moves forward with his right foot. You are standing in Nakado Kamae with your Shinai held diagonally and your heels together.

乙 Otsu
You

甲 Koh
Attacker

2. Your Attacker steps forward with his right foot and cuts to Makko, the Top of Your Head. You respond by blocking with your sword in Chudan Kamae as you step back with your left foot.

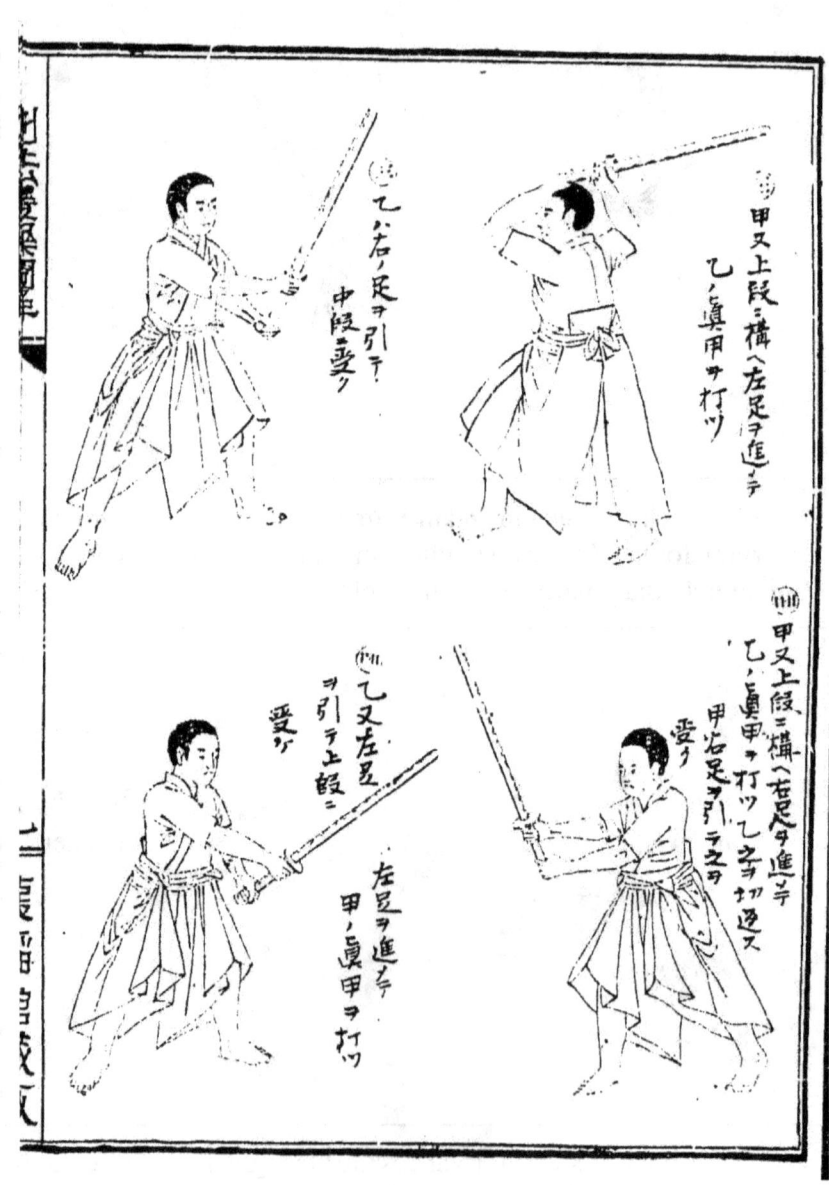

Jodan Kake 上段掛 Attacked from Upper Stance Steps 3 ~ 4

乙 Otsu
You

甲 Koh
Attacker

3. The Attacker again goes into Jodan Kamae, steps forward with his left foot and cuts to Makko. You respond by pulling your right foot back and blocking with your sword in Chudan Kamae.

乙 Otsu
You

甲 Koh
Attacker

4. Once again, the Attacker goes into Jodan Kamae and, stepping forward with his right foot, cuts to Makko. You again pull your left foot back and block this strike with your sword held in Jodan Kamae. Next, step forward with your left foot do a Kiri Kaeshi, Switching from Block to Strike, cutting to the Attacker's Makko. The Attacker pulls his right foot back and blocks.

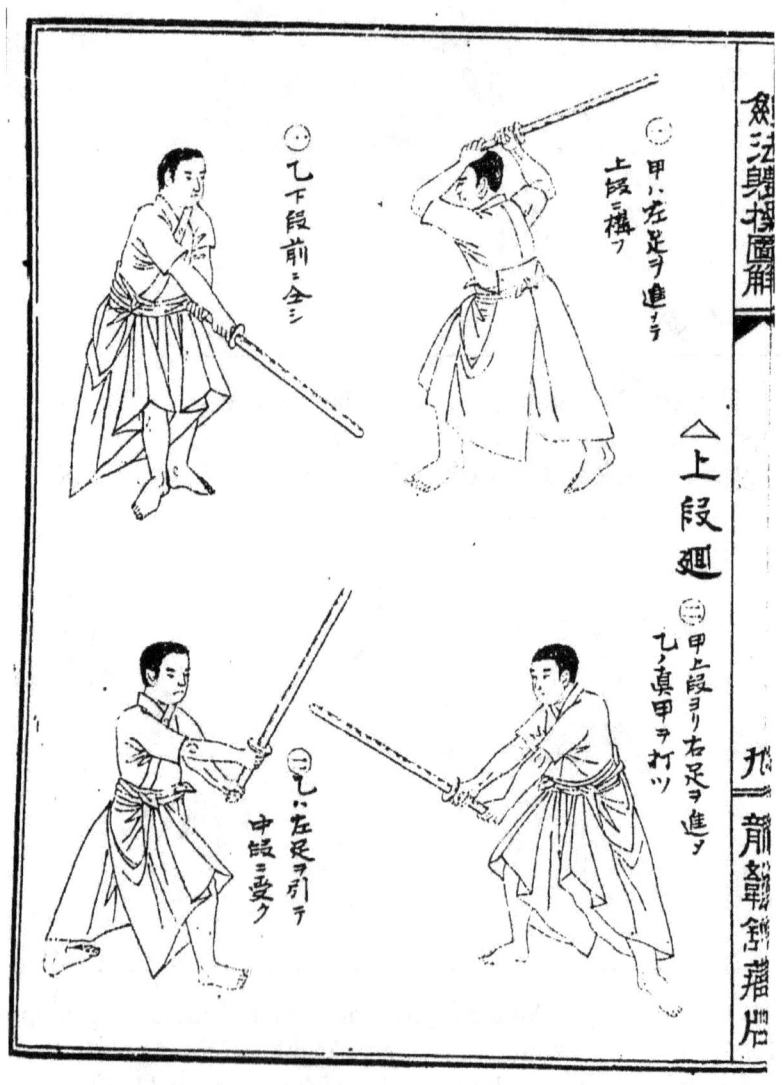

Jodan Mawashi 上段廻 Revolving from Jodan Steps 1 ~ 2

乙 Otsu
You

甲 Koh
Attacker

1. The Attacker is in Jodan Kamae and moves forward with his left foot. You are in Gedan Kamae, with your heels together in the same way done in the previous technique.

乙 Otsu
You

甲 Koh
Attacker

2. The Attacker steps forward with his right foot and cuts to your Makko. You respond by pulling your left foot back and blocking with your sword in Chudan Kamae.

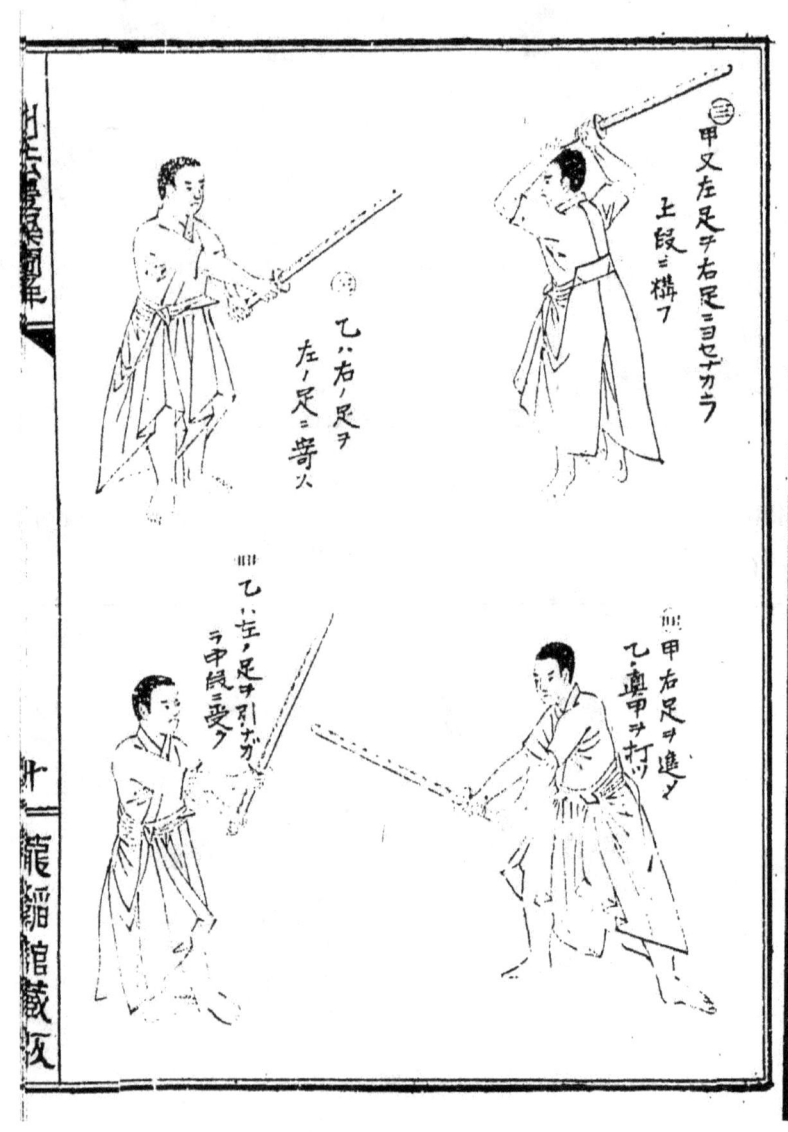

Jodan Mawashi 上段廻 Revolving from Jodan Steps 3 ~ 4

3. The Attacker returns to Jodan Kamae and pulls his left foot up beside his right. You pull your right foot beside your left.

4. The Attacker steps forward with his right foot and cuts to Makko. You respond by pulling back your left foot and blocking with your sword held in Chudan Kamae.

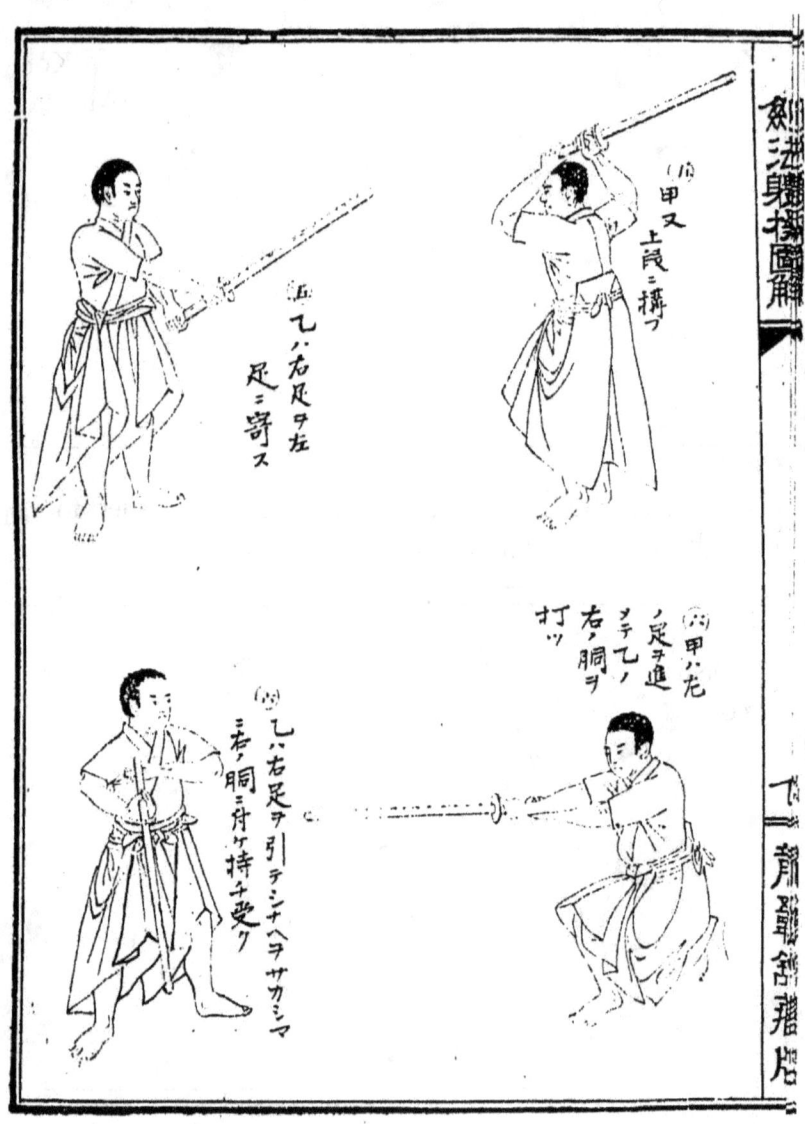

Jodan Mawashi 上段廻 Revolving from Jodan Steps 5 ~ 6

乙 Otsu
You

甲 Koh
Attacker

5. Pulling his feet together, the Attacker goes into Jodan again.
You slide your right foot towards your left foot.

乙 Otsu
You

甲 Koh
Attacker

6. The attacker steps forward with his left foot and cuts your Migi
Do, Right Side. You defend against this cut by pulling your right
foot back, reversing your Shinai and holding it against your right
side. This will block the Attacker's cut.

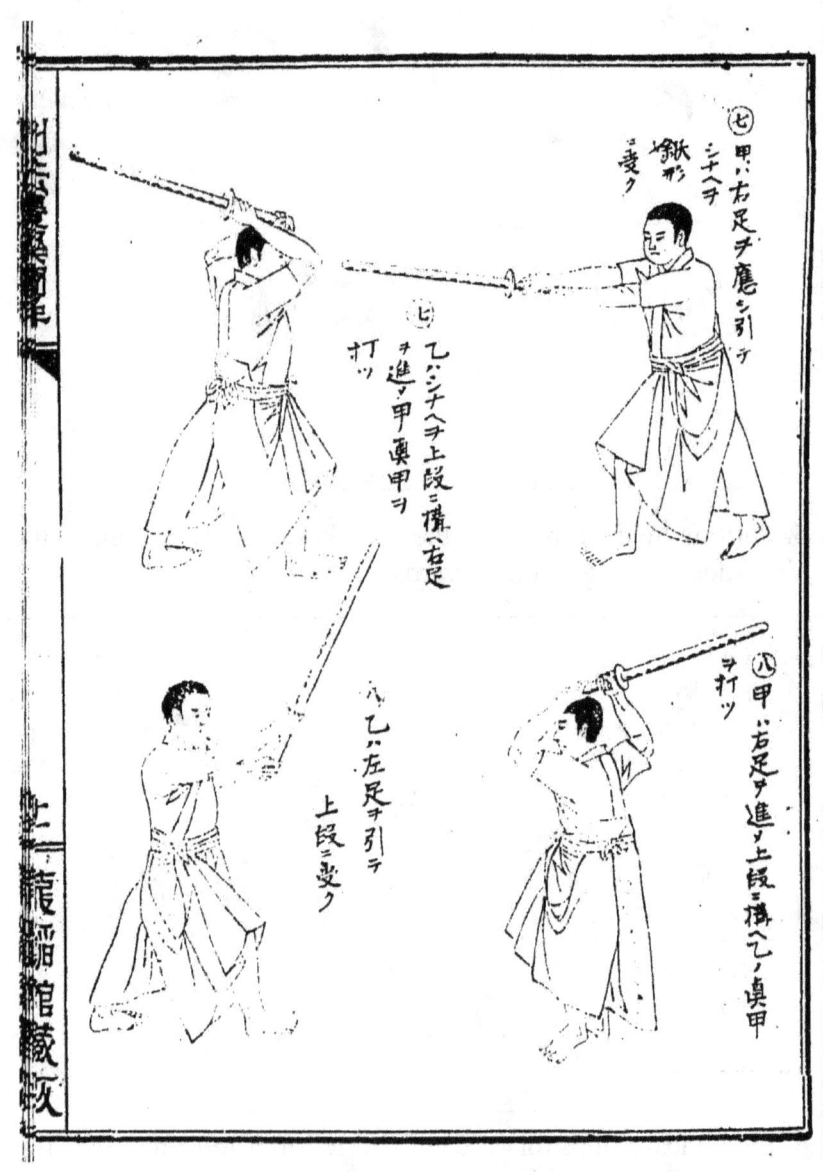

Jodan Mawashi 上段廻 Revolving from Jodan Steps 7 ~ 8

乙 Otsu
You

甲 Koh
Attacker

7. Raising your Shinai into Jodan Kamae, step forward with your right foot and cut to Makko. Your opponent responds by pulling his right foot back slightly and blocking with his sword held in Kuwagata Kamae.

乙 Otsu
You

甲 Koh
Attacker

8. The Attacker pulls his feet together and goes into Jodan Kamae. The then steps forward with his right foot and cuts to Makko. You respond by pulling your left foot back and blocking with your sword in Jodan Kamae.

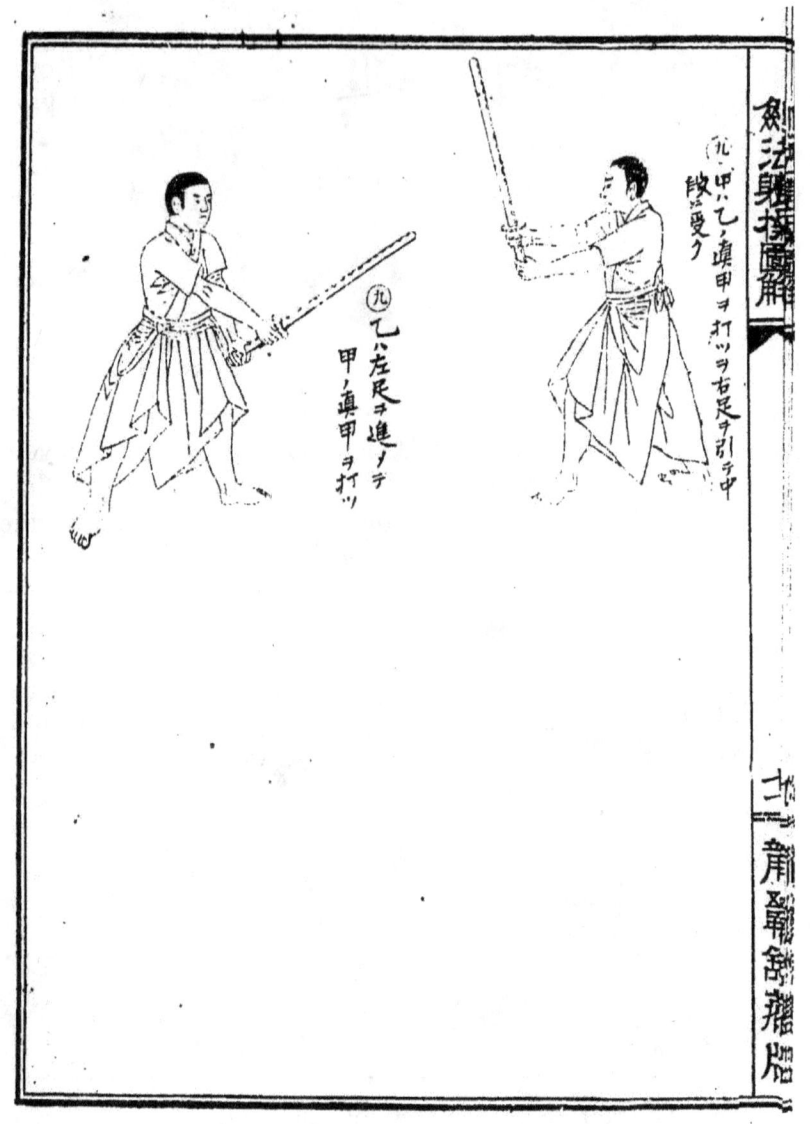

Jodan Mawashi 上段廻 Revolving from Jodan Step 9

乙 Otsu
You

甲 Koh
Attacker

9. Next, you step forward with your left foot and cut to the Attacker's Makko. He responds to your cut to his head by stepping back with his right foot and blocking with his sword held in Chudan Kamae.

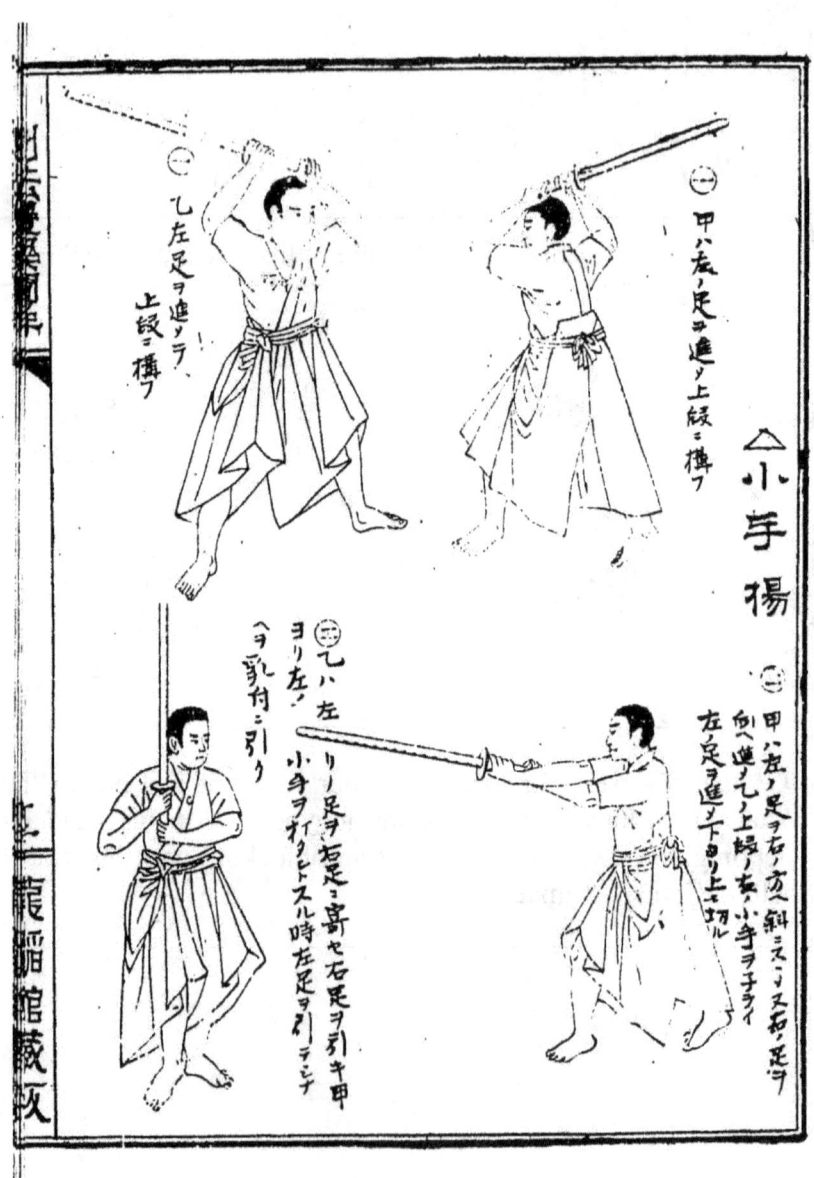

Koteage 小手揚 Raising the Hands Steps 1 ~ 2

乙 Otsu
You

甲 Koh
Attacker

1. The Attacker stands in Jodan Kamae and advances with his left foot forward. Your stand in Jodan and advance with your left foot forward.

乙 Otsu
You

甲 Koh
Attacker

2. The Attacker steps diagonally to the right with his left foot. You respond by pulling your left foot back beside your right. Next, he steps directly toward you with his right foot. In response, you pull your right foot back. The Attacker, stepping forward with his left foot, cuts up from below aiming for your left arm, which is holding your sword in Jodan Kamae. This cut is called Kote Uchi, Cut to the Hands. You evade by sliding your left foot back and taking Chizuke Kamae by pulling your sword to your nipple.

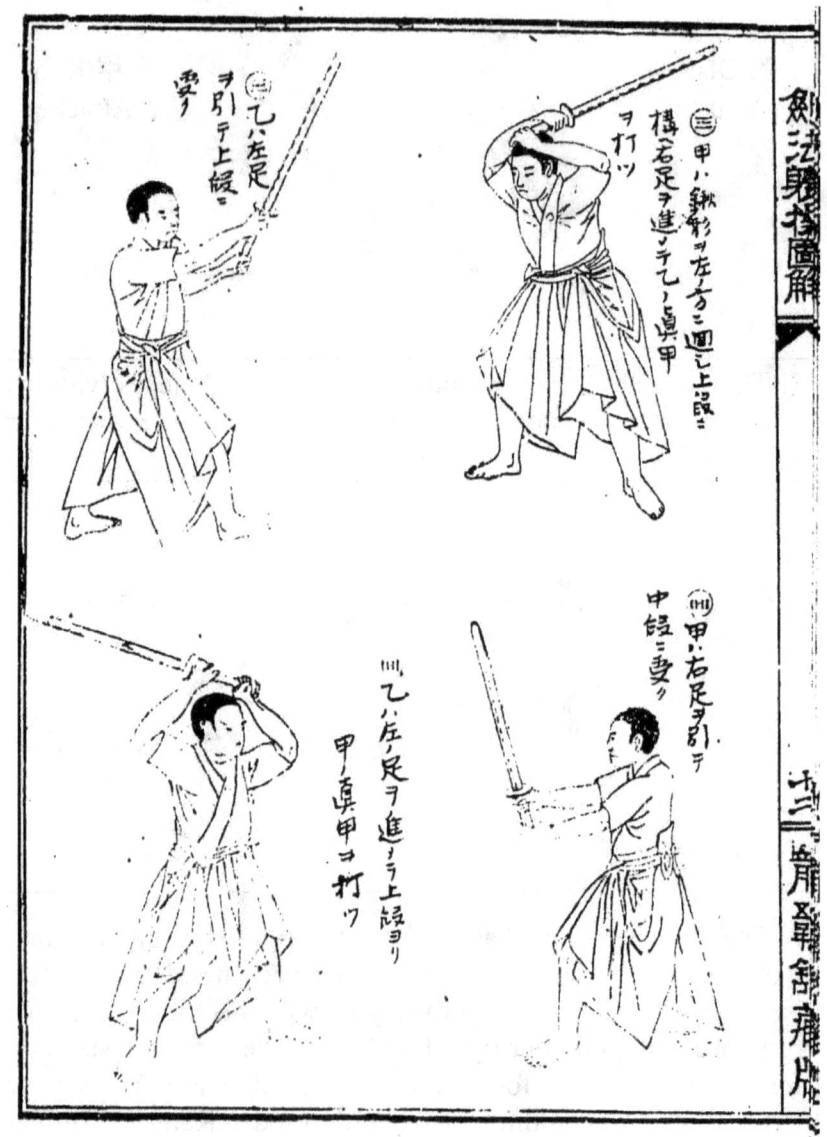

Koteage 小手揚 Raising the Hands Steps 3 ~ 4

乙 Otsu
You

甲 Koh
Attacker

3. The Attacker rotates his sword to the left shifting from Kuwagata Kamae to Jodan Kamae. Stepping forward with his right foot he cuts to your Makko. You respond by pulling your left foot back and blocking with your sword in Jodan Kamae. Note: I presume after the previous upward cut you ended in Kuwagata Kamae.

乙 Otsu
You

甲 Koh
Attacker

4. You follow up by stepping forward with your left foot and cutting down on your opponent's Makko from Jodan Kamae. The Attacker pulls his left foot back and blocks your strike with his sword held in Chudan Kamae.

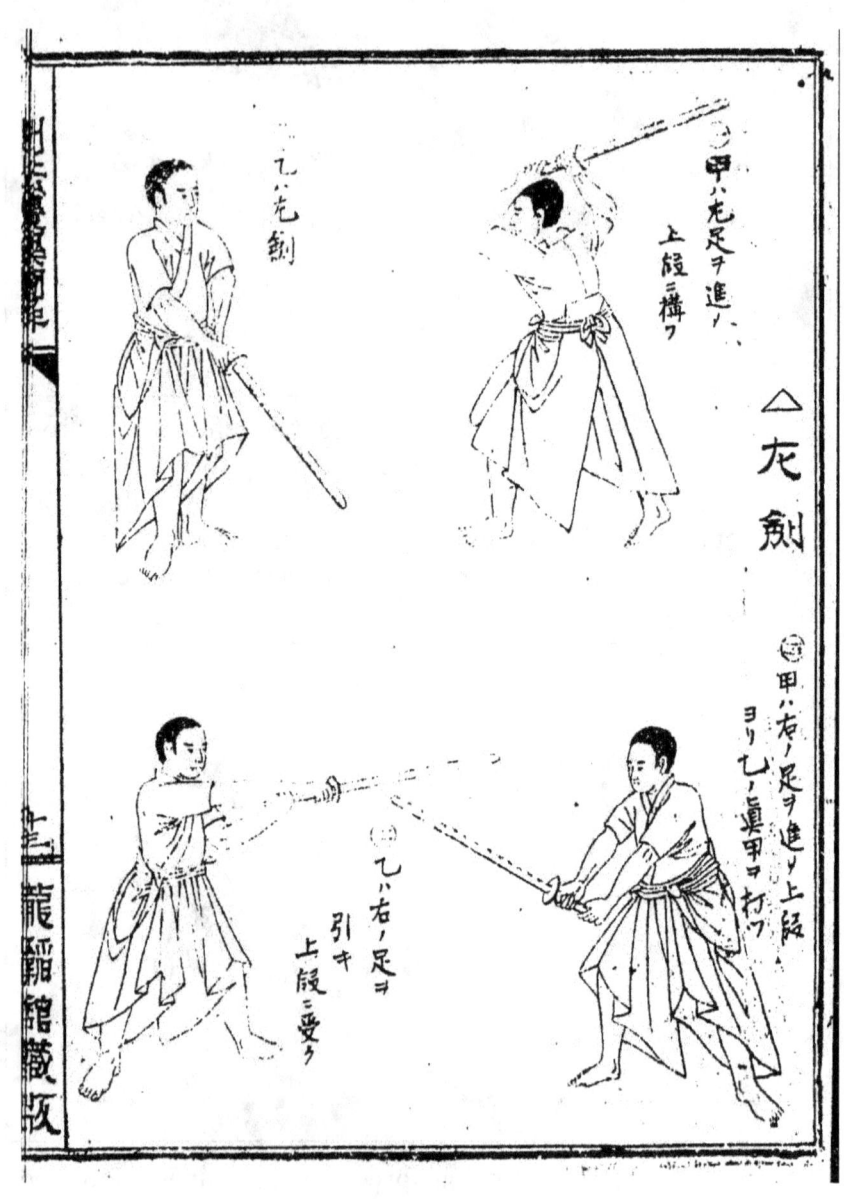

Saken 左劍 Left Sword Steps 1 ~ 2

乙 Otsu
You

甲 Koh
Attacker

△
左
劍

1. The Attacker stands in Jodan Kamae and advances with his left foot forward. You are in Saken Kamae.

乙 Otsu
You

甲 Koh
Attacker

2. Next, the Attacker steps forward with his right foot and cuts down from Jodan Kamae to Makko. You respond by pulling your right foot back and blocking with your sword held in Jodan Kamae.

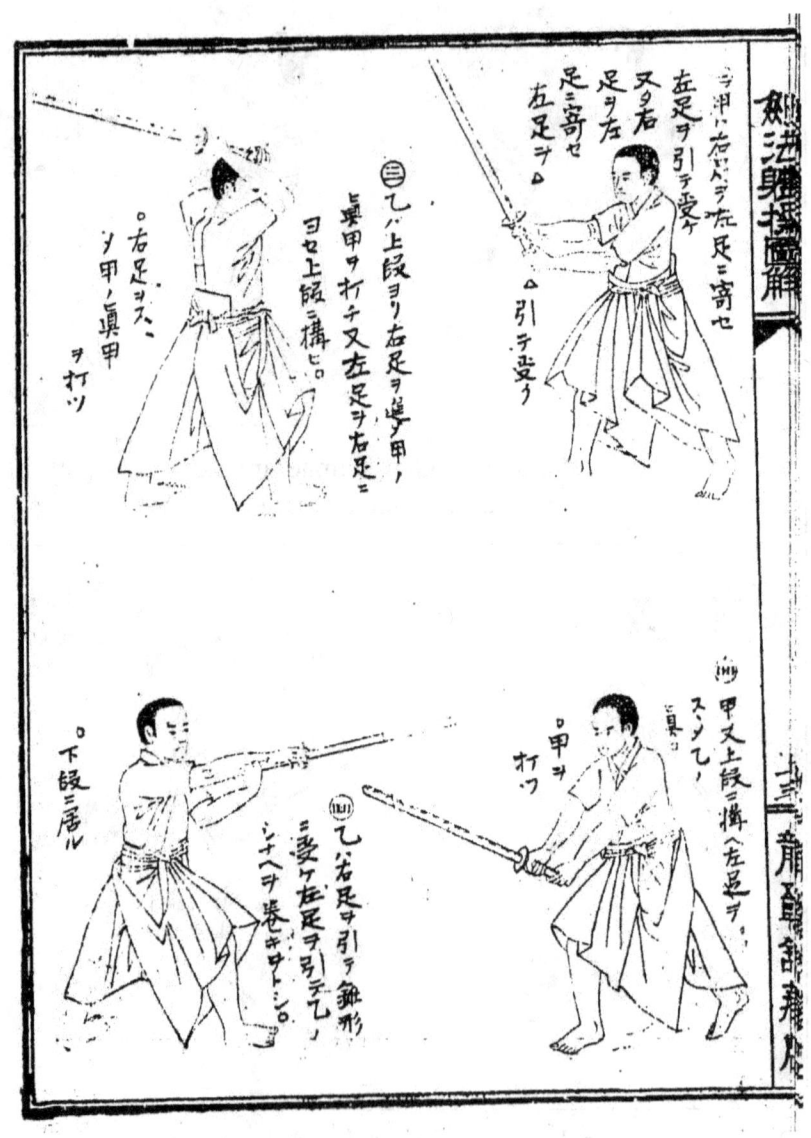

Saken 左劍 Left Sword Steps 3 ~ 4

乙 Otsu
You

甲 Koh
Attacker

3. You then step forward with your right foot and cut to the top of your opponent's head. The Attacker avoids this by pulling his right foot back beside his left, then stepping back with his left foot.   You then draw your left foot up to your right foot and return to Jodan Kamae. Stepping forward with your right foot cut again to the top of your opponent's head. Your opponent again draws his right foot back to his left foot then steps back with his left foot and blocks your cut with his sword held in Jodan Kamae.

乙 Otsu
You

甲 Koh
Attacker

4. The Attacker steps forward with his left foot and cuts down from Jodan Kamae to the top of your head.   You respond by pulling your right foot back and blocking this cut with your sword held in Kuwagata Kamae. Next, drawing your left foot back force your opponent's sword down with a Maki Otoshi, Wrap and Drop, then take Gedan Kamae.

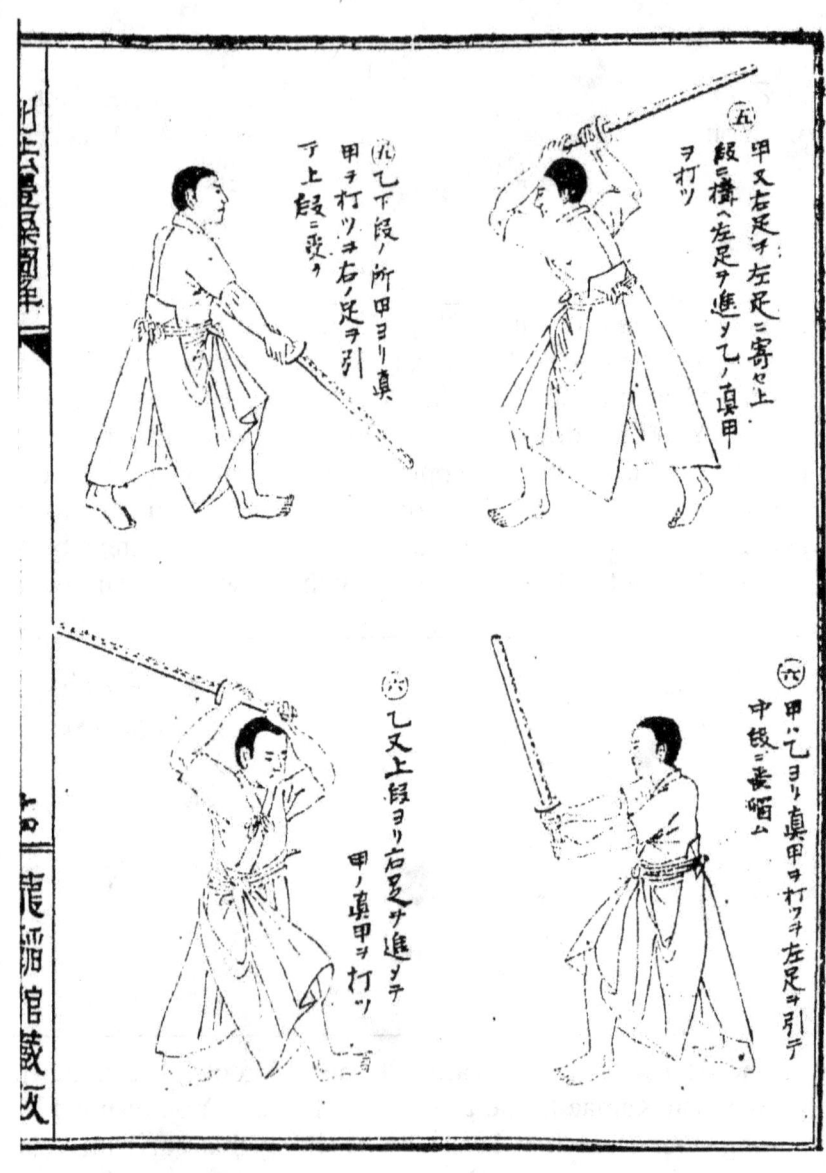

Saken 左劍 Left Sword Steps 5 ~ 6

乙 Otsu
You

甲 Koh
Attacker

5. The attacker draws his right foot up until it is beside his left foot and goes into Jodan Kamae. You are in Gedan Kamae. He then steps forward with his left foot and cuts to the top of your head. You respond by pulling your right foot back and blocking your opponent's cut with your sword in Jodan Kamae.

乙 Otsu
You

甲 Koh
Attacker

6. You then step forward with your right foot and cut down to Makko from Jodan Kamae. Your opponent responds to your cut to the top of his head by pulling his left leg back and doing an Uke Tome, Block and Stop, with his sword held in Chudan Kamae.

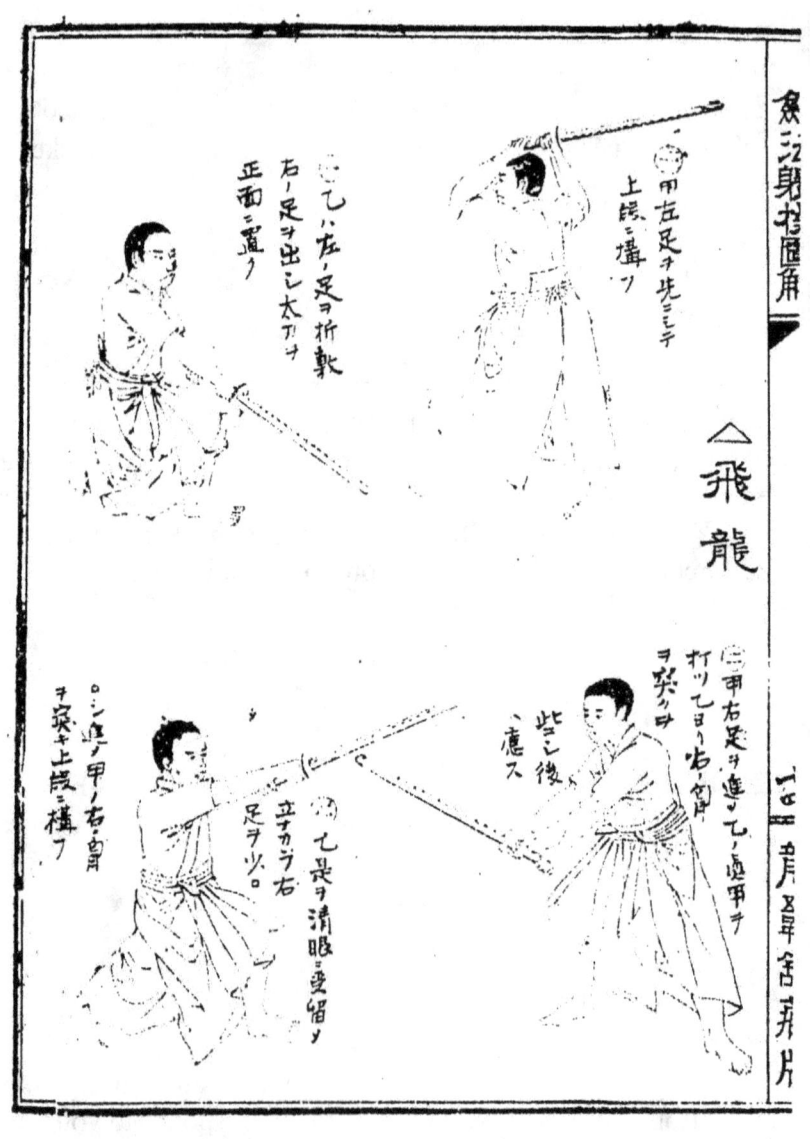

Hiryu 飛龍 Flying Dragon Steps 1 ~ 2

1. The Attacker stands in Jodan Kamae with his left foot forward. You are kneeling on the ground in a stance called Oshiki, Bend and Spread. This means your left knee is bent and on the ground while your right leg is upright with your foot facing your opponent. Your sword is extended out in front of you.

2. The Attacker moves forward with his right foot and cuts to the top of your head. You defend against this attack by doing an Uke Tome, Block and Stop, with your sword held in Seigan Kamae. Next, stand up and take a short step forward with your right foot and stab your opponent in the right side of his chest. Your opponent dodges back away from this attack. Next, you shift into Jodan Kamae.

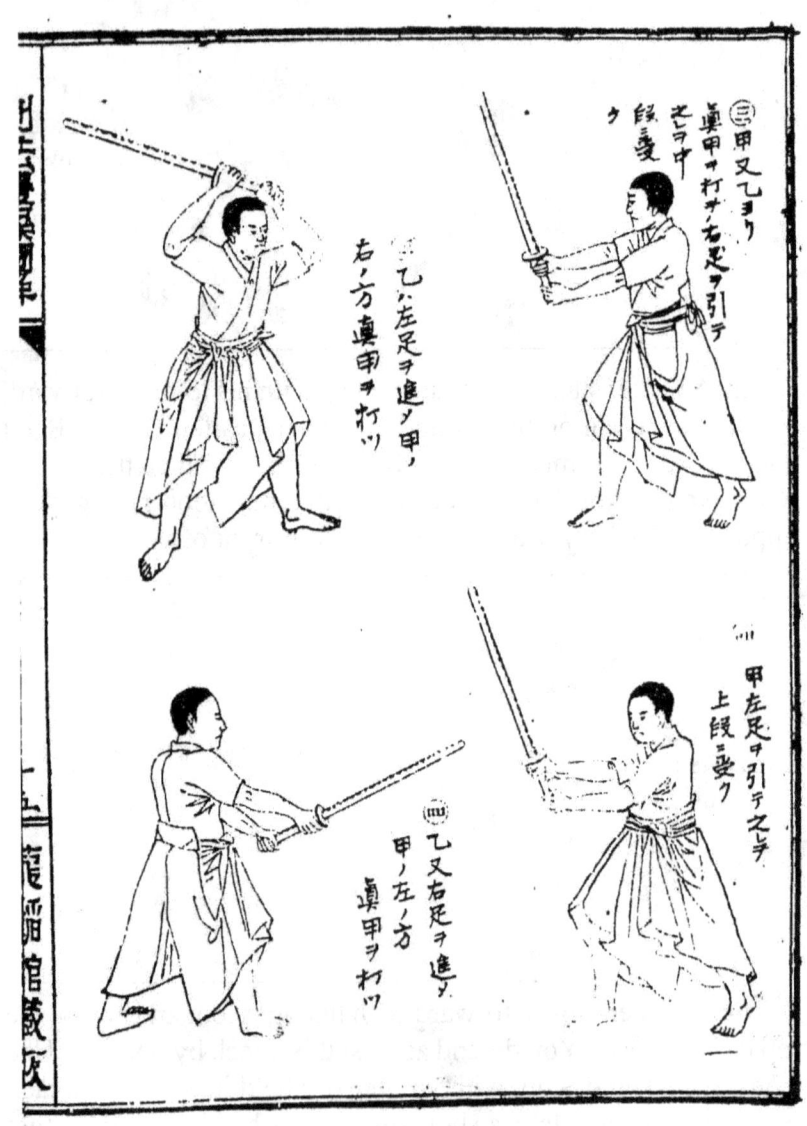

Hiryu 飛龍 Flying Dragon Steps 3 ~ 4

乙 Otsu
You

甲 Koh
Attacker

3. Take a step forward with your left foot and cut to the right side of your opponent's head. He responds by pulling his right foot back and blocking with his sword held in Chudan Kamae.

乙 Otsu
You

甲 Koh
Attacker

4. Next, step forward with your right foot and cut to the left side of the Attacker's head. He responds by pulling his left foot back and blocking with his sword held in Jodan Kamae.

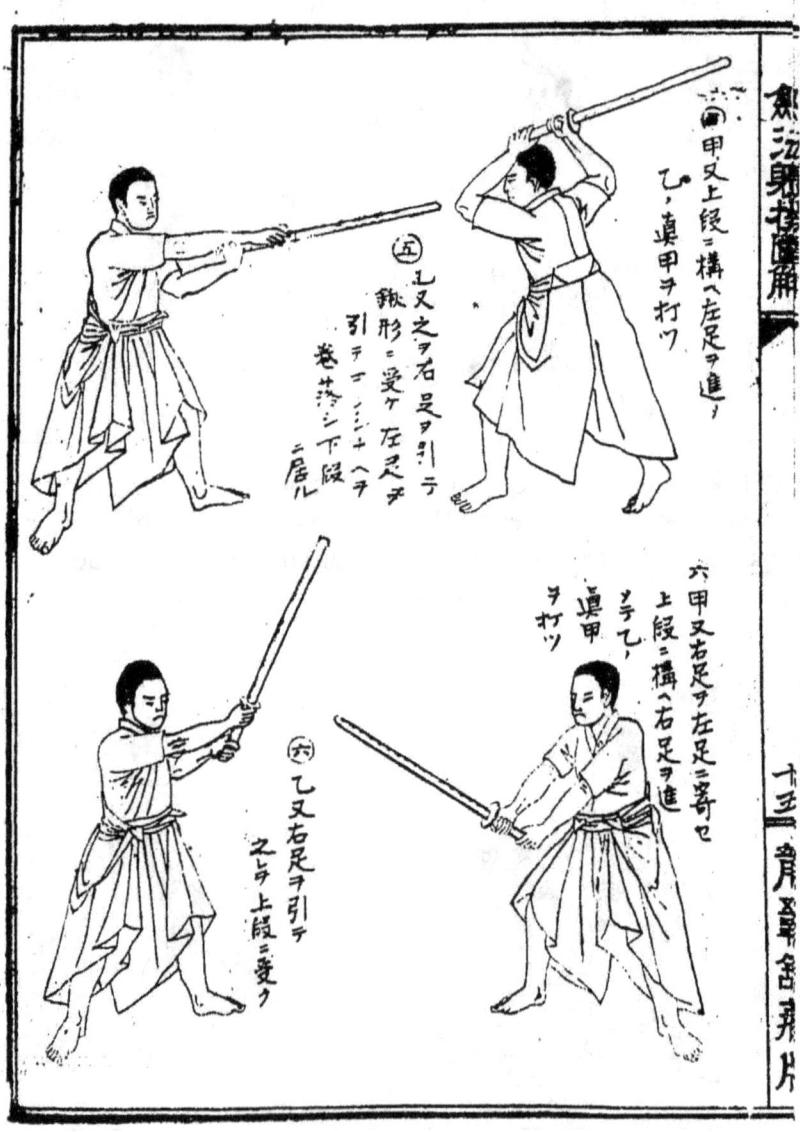

Koteage 小手揚 Raising the Hands Steps 5 ~ 6

乙 Otsu
You

甲 Koh
Attacker

5. The Attacker goes into Jodan Kamae and, stepping forward with his left foot, cuts to the top of your head. In response you pull your right foot back and block his attack with your sword held in Kuwagata Kamae. Next, as you pull your left foot back, do a Maki Otoshi, wrapping up and forcing down your opponent's Shinai with your own. At the end of this move you should be in in Gedan Kamae.

乙 Otsu
You

甲 Koh
Attacker

6. The Attacker responds by sliding his right foot up beside his left and going into Jodan Kame. He then steps forward with his right foot and cuts to the top of your head. You respond by pulling your right foot back and going into Jodan Kamae.

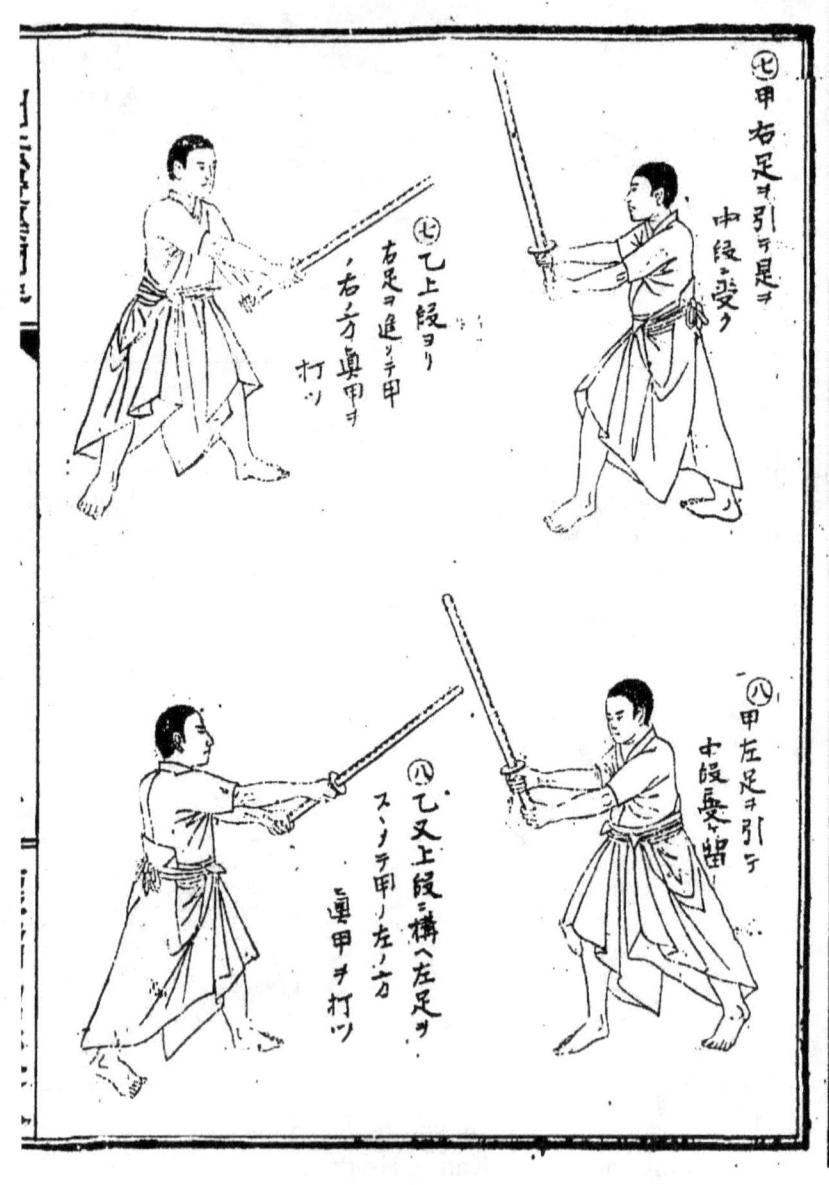

Koteage 小手揚 Raising the Hands Steps 7 ~ 8

乙 Otsu
You

甲 Koh
Attacker

7. From Jodan Kamae you step forward with your right foot and cut to the right side of the Attacker's head. He responds by stepping back with his right foot and blocking with his sword in Chudan Kamae.

乙 Otsu
You

甲 Koh
Attacker

8. You return to Jodan Kamae and, stepping forward with your left foot, cut to the left side of your opponent's head. He responds by pulling his left leg back and doing an Uke Tome, Block and Stop, with his sword in Chudan Kamae.

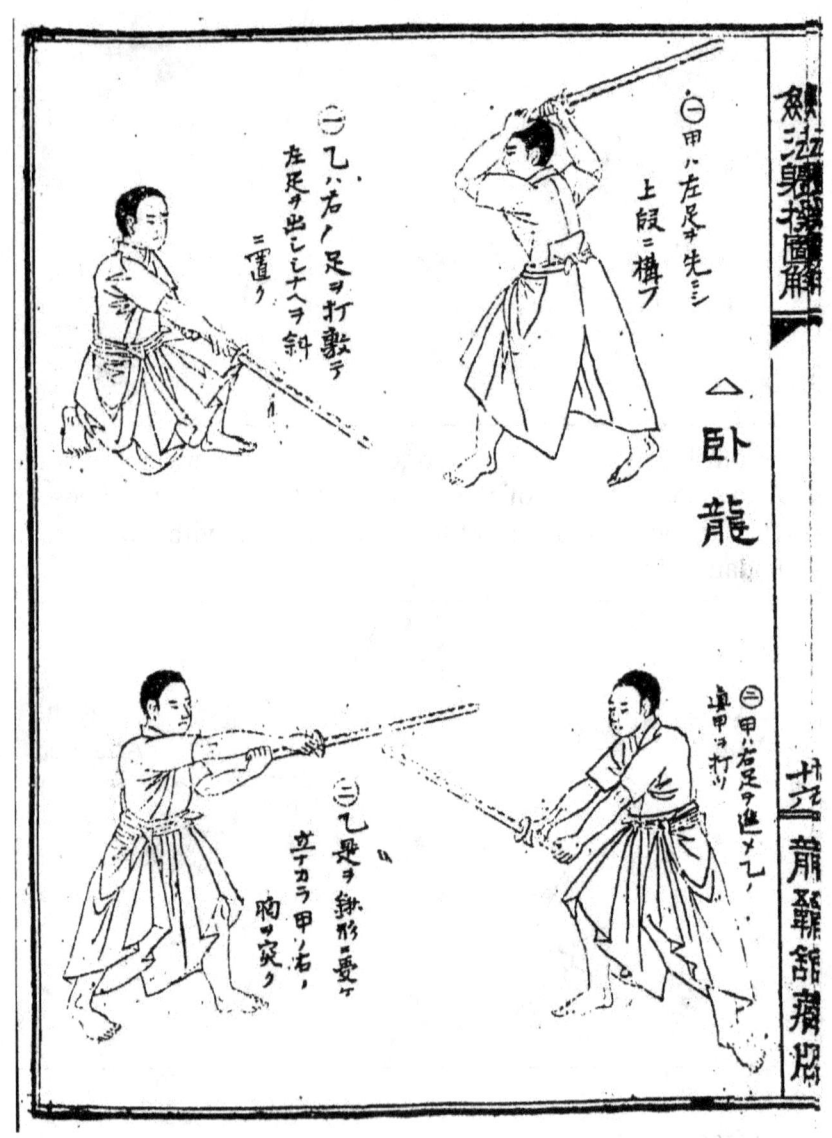

○甲ハ左足ヲ先ニシ
上段ニ横フ

（一）乙ハ右ノ足ヲ打敷テ
左足ヲ出シナヘヲ斜
ニ置ク

△臥
龍

（三）甲ハ右足ヲ進メ乙ノ
真甲ヲ打リ

（二）乙是ヲ鉢形ニ要ケ
立テカラ甲ノ右ノ
胸ニ突ク

剣法躬樣圖解

廿九　蒲龍舘藏版

Garyou 臥龍 Prone Dragon Steps 1 ~ 2

乙 Otsu
You

甲 Koh
Attacker

1. The Attacker stands in Jodan Kamae with his left foot forward. You are kneeling on the ground in a stance called Oshiki, Bend and Spread. This means your right knee is on the ground, while your left leg is upright with your foot facing your opponent. Your sword is extended diagonally out in front of you.

乙 Otsu
You

甲 Koh
Attacker

2. The Attacker steps forward with his right foot and cuts to the top of your head. You respond by blocking with your sword in Kuwagata. Next, as you stand up, stab to the right side of your opponent's chest.

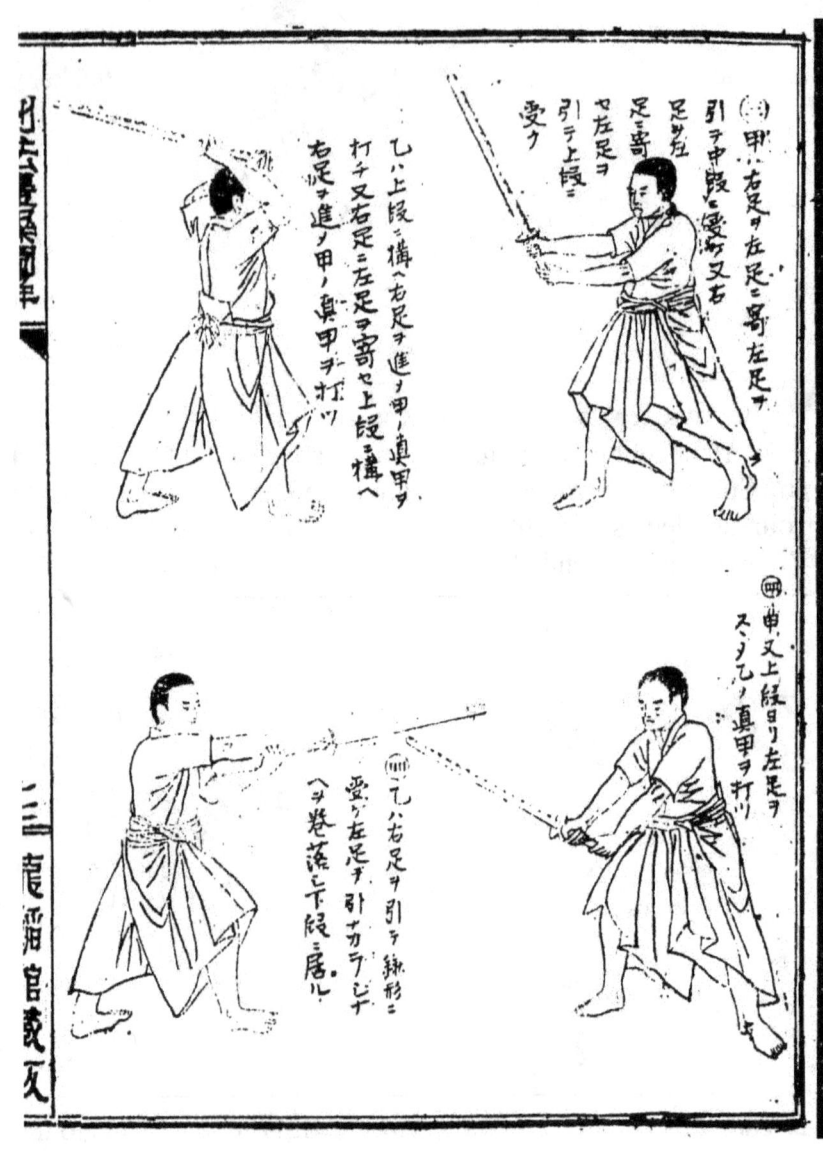

Garyou 臥龍 Prone Dragon Steps 3 ~ 4

乙 Otsu
You

甲 Koh
Attacker

3. Stepping forward with your right foot cut down onto the top of the Attacker's head from Jodan Kamae. The Attacker responds by sliding his right foot back so it is beside his left. He then pulls his left foot back and blocks your attack with his sword in Chudan Kamae. You then slide your right foot back so it is beside your left foot and, with your sword in Jodan Kamae, again step forward with your right foot and cut to the top of the Attacker's head. He defends by pulling his right foot back to his left foot and then steps back with his left foot as he blocks with his sword in Jodan Kamae.

乙 Otsu
You

甲 Koh
Attacker

4. The Attacker steps forward with his left foot and cuts the top of your head. You respond by pulling your right leg back and blocking with your sword in Kuwagata Kamae. Next, while stepping back with your left foot do a Maki Otoshi, wrapping up your opponent's Shinai with your own, then forcing it down and going into Gedan Kamae.

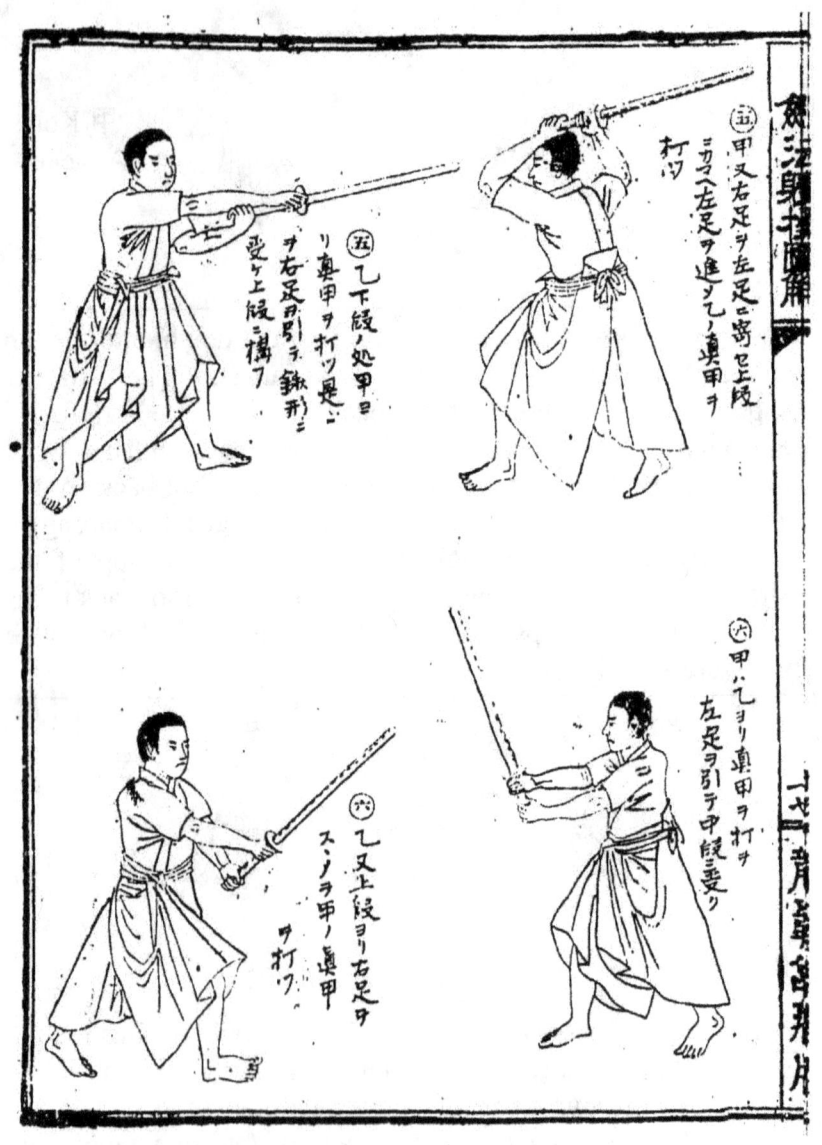

Garyou 臥龍 Prone Dragon Steps 5 ~ 6

乙 Otsu
You

甲 Koh
Attacker

5. Next the Attacker slides his right foot beside his left foot, then steps forward with his left foot cutting to the top of your head. From Gedan Kamae, you pull your right foot back and block the Attacker's cut with your sword in Kuwagata Kamae. You then raise your sword into Jodan Kamae.

乙 Otsu
You

甲 Koh
Attacker

6. Stepping forward with your right foot you cut down from Jodan Kamae to your opponent's head. Your opponent responds to your attack by pulling his right foot back and blocking with his sword in Chudan Kamae.

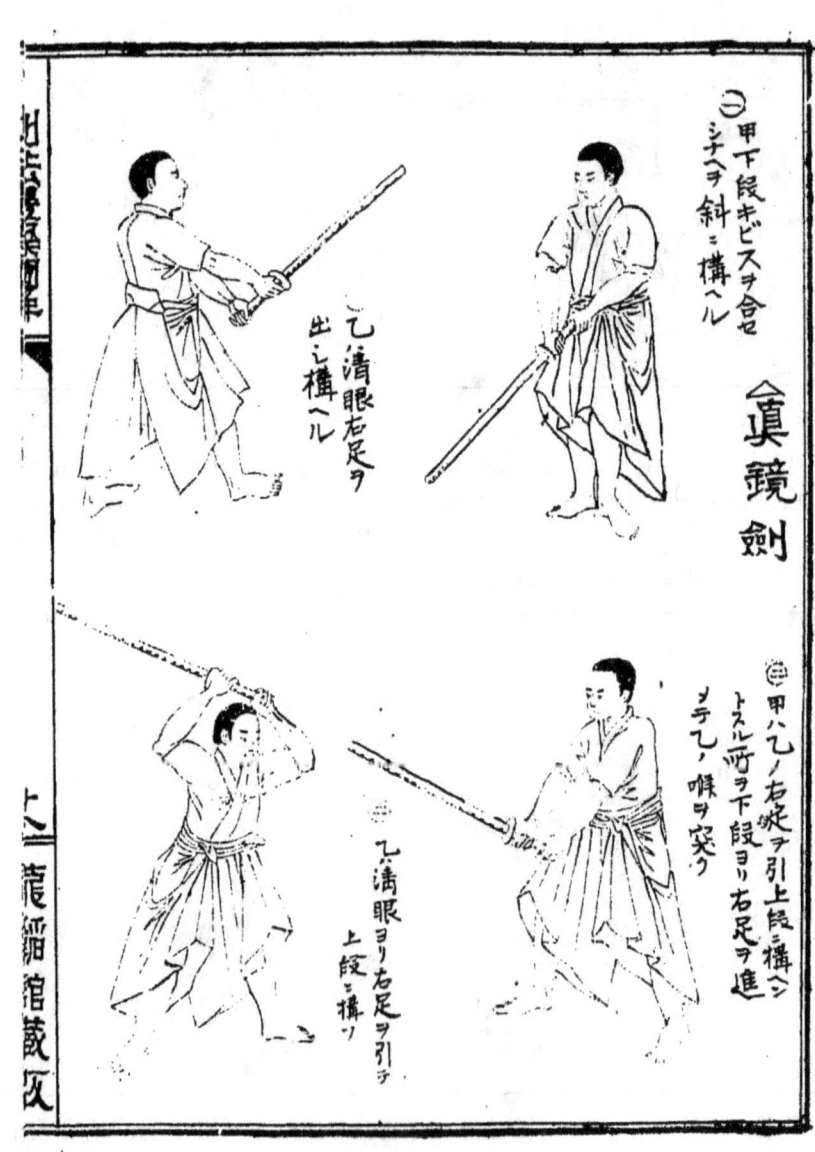

Shinkyo 真鏡 True Mirror　Steps 1 ~ 2

乙 Otsu
You

甲 Koh
Attacker

1. The Attacker stands with his heels together and his sword held in Gedan Kamae. You are standing in Seigan Kamae with your right foot forward.

乙 Otsu
You

甲 Koh
Attacker

2. You begin to pull your right foot back and start to switch from Seigan Kamae to Jodan Kamae. As you begin this move the Attacker steps forward with his right foot and stabs to your throat.

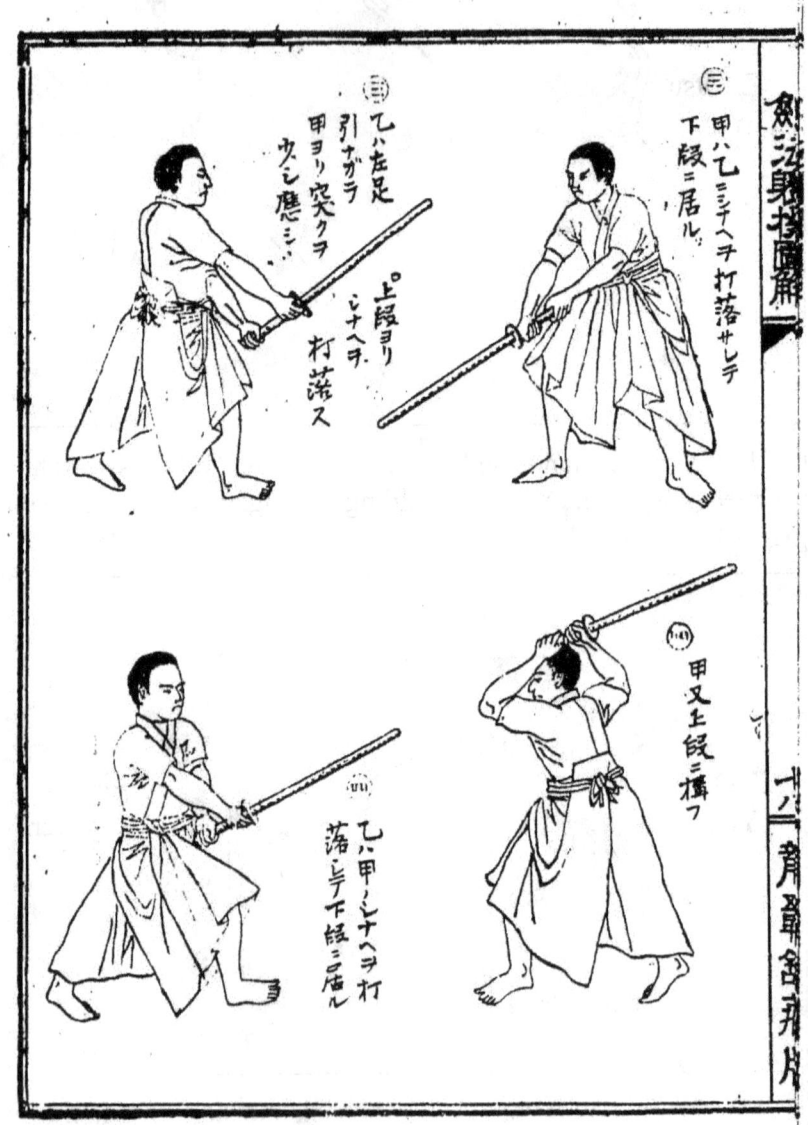

Shinkyo 真鏡 True Mirror　Steps 3 ~ 4

乙 Otsu
You

甲 Koh
Attacker

3. You respond to this Tsuki, or Stab, by pulling your left foot back and twisting away. From Jodan you counter-attack with a Uchi Otoshi, Strike and Drop, to your opponent's Shinai. The Attacker responds to your Uchi Otoshi by taking Gedan Kamae.

乙 Otsu
You

甲 Koh
Attacker

4. After striking your opponent's sword down with a Uchi Otoshi you take Gedan Kamae (Note: The illustration shows Chudan Kamae.) Your opponent raises his sword into Jodan Kamae.

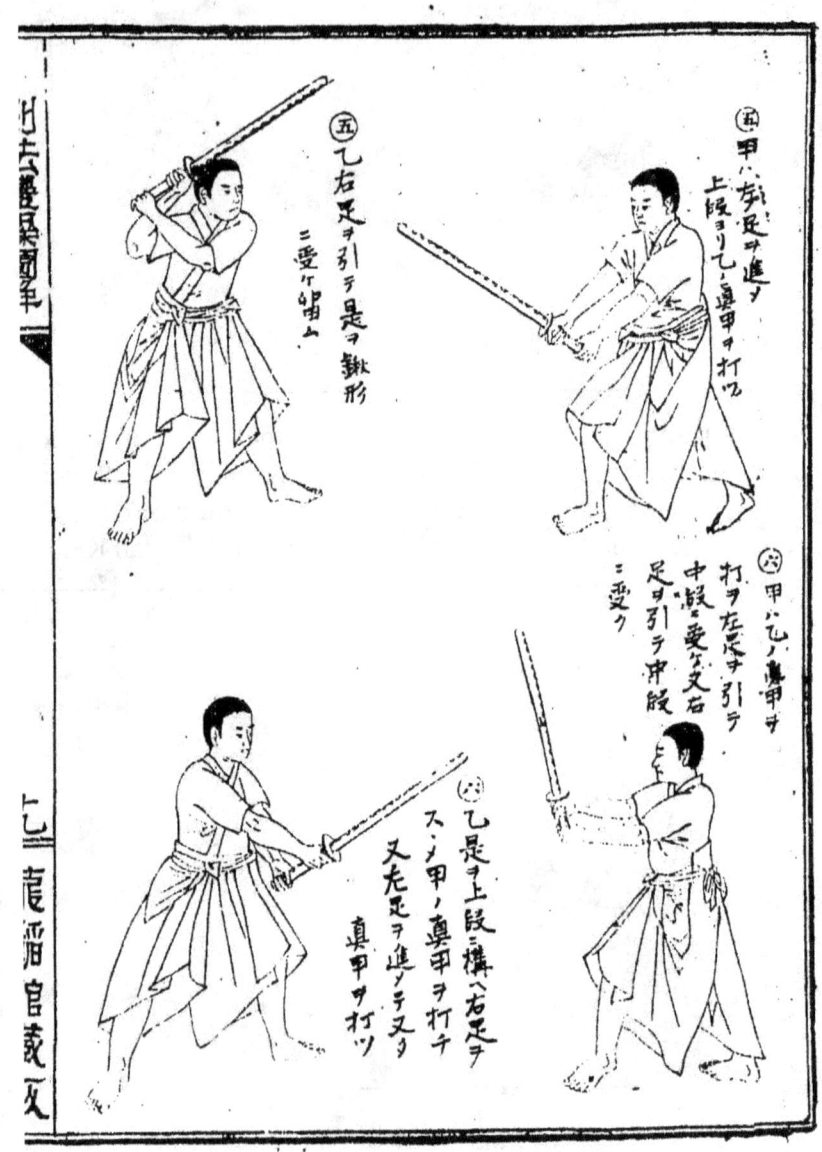

Shinkyo 真鏡 True Mirror   Steps 5 ~ 6

乙 Otsu
You

甲 Koh
Attacker

5. The Attacker steps forward with his left foot and cuts your head from Jodan Kamae. You respond by pulling your right foot back and defending with Uke Tome, Block and Stop, with your sword in Kuwagata Kamae.

乙 Otsu
You

甲 Koh
Attacker

6. You then counter-attack by switching to Jodan Kamae, stepping forward with your right foot and cutting to the top of the Attacker's head. The Attacker responds to your attack by pulling his left foot back and blocking with his sword in Chudan Kamae. You attack again by stepping forward with your left foot and cutting to the top of his head. Your opponent steps back with his right foot and blocks with his sword held in Chudan Kamae.

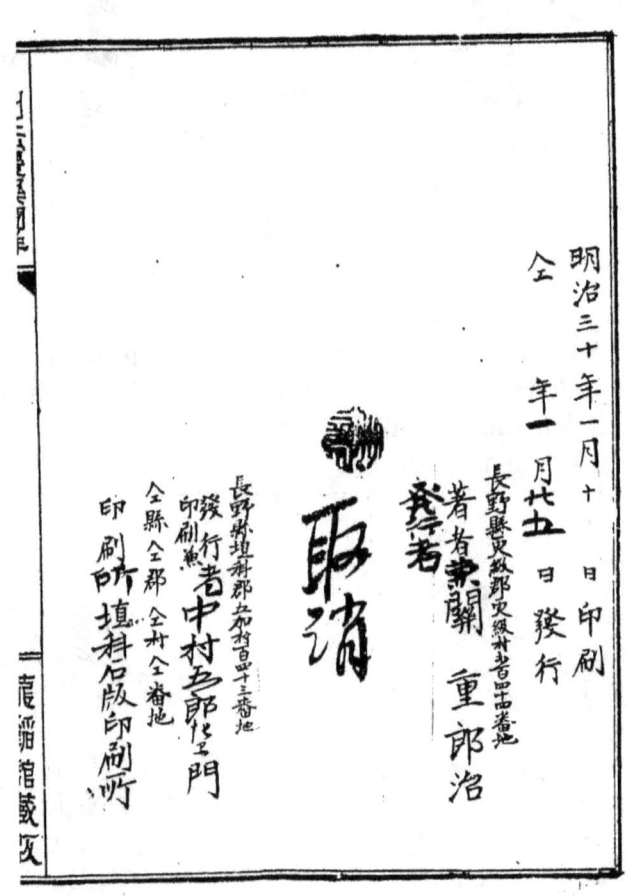

**PUBLISHED JANUARY 25ᵀᴴ OF MEIJI 30 1897
NAGANO PREFECTURE
AUTHOR AND EDITOR: SEKI JUROJI**

www.ingramcontent.com/pod-product-compliance
Lightning Source LLC
Chambersburg PA
CBHW072201270326
41930CB00011B/2499